"This book is a must-read for anyone who has ever felt desperate, hopeless, marginalized, or 'beyond saving.' It's also a reminder of how our environments and self-images can trigger substance abuse and addiction, often without us even realizing it until it's nearly too late. Most of all, however, it's a reminder that it's actually *never* too late to marshal your inner strength and lean on the people who love you to live the life you want. Simply put, Mark's story is a reminder that we are all authors, and heroes, of our own stories."

—Dominic Nicosia, Recovery Unplugged Treatment Centers

"For so many who are caught in the crosshairs of faith and sexual orientation, 'religion' can be deadly. Incredibly personal, poignant, deeply tragic, and yet ultimately triumphant, Mark Turnipseed's extraordinary memoir *My Suicide Race* should be mandatory reading for anyone who has struggled with addiction, internalized homophobia, or faced any other mental health challenges which caused them to question who God made them to be."

—Daniel G. Karslake, critically acclaimed director and producer of *For the Bible Tells Me So* and *For They Know Not What They Do*

"Mark Turnipseed's *My Suicide Race* is a harrowing roller-coaster ride of a read, full of unexpected twists, turns, and bone-chilling drops. Charting one man's emotional journey from childhood to rock-bottom addict, you'll cheer as Turnipseed finally faces his demons by reaching deep into his soul, finding redemption in his children, and embracing his true self."

—Kergan Edwards-Stout, award-winning author of *Never Turn Your Back on the Tide* and *Songs for the New Depression*

"Look up 'hero's journey,' and see the face of this young man who conquered addiction through triathlon training and named himself proudly as gay. It's painfully and joyfully told in this remarkably honest book."

—Brian McNaught, author of *On Being Gay* and *Now That I'm Out, What Do I Do?*

MY SUICIDE RACE

MY SUICIDE RACE

*WINNING OVER THE TRAUMA
OF ADDICTION, RECOVERY,
AND COMING OUT*

A MEMOIR

MARK A. TURNIPSEED

ISBN: 978-1-7360219-0-3 (paperback)
ISBN: 978-1-7360219-1-0 (ebook)

Library of Congress Control Number: 2020921245

Cover: Design: Russell Noe / Photograph: Danny Cardozo
        Stylist: Collin Ridgway / Model: Mark A. Turnipseed
        Headshots: Photographer: Andre Gabb
Interior Design: Sun Editing & Book Design (suneditwrite.com)

Printed and bound in the USA.

The author of this book does not dispense medical advice or prescribe the use of any technique as a form of treatment for physical, emotional, or medical problems without the advice of a physician, either directly or indirectly. The intent of the author is only to offer information of a general nature based on his own experience. In the event you use any of the information in this book for yourself, the author and the publisher assume no responsibility for your actions.

Some names of individuals in this book have been changed to protect their anonymity.

*This book is dedicated to the addict who still suffers
and the people who love them, that they
both may find hope in my story.*

TABLE OF CONTENTS

Introduction

M y lies began when I was six years old, and throughout my childhood and many years of my adult life, I tried to build a house on a foundation of those lies.

So this book is for all the liars out there, especially the ones who think they have it all figured out. It's for the liars who think they are the shit and the ones who believe they're no good. It's for the family man or mother who doesn't believe their son looks up to them and for the gay man or woman who thinks they can't tell the truth about who they are.

It's also for the people who love the liars and who have been hurt by those lies. For far too long, my lies caused pain and tears to those I loved.

As you continue reading, you'll learn about my lies and my addictions—substances that allowed me to avoid pairing actions and consequences together. Substances that put me in a black hole where morals didn't exist, making it possible for me to bypass the experience of remorse. I now recognize that my first impulse was to shove guilt under the rug and act out in anger and frustration because I was so scared my lies would be found out—that my true identity would be revealed. I thought: *People will know I'm a drug addict. People will know I'm a thief. People will know I'm a hedonist. And the scariest of all, people will know I'm gay.*

Melody Beattie, one of my favorite authors, dissects the difference between guilt and shame in her book, *The Art of Letting Go*. She describes "guilt" as the feeling that what we *did* wasn't okay, but "shame" is the feeling that *who we are* isn't okay.

Starting from a young age, I felt immense guilt about who I was, but over time, shame took over—the belief that it wasn't just what I did that was wrong. *I* was wrong. *Who I was* wasn't okay. It was so painful that I had to do anything I could to dissociate myself from it. As a child, I intuitively turned to different strategies like obsessive-compulsive behavior. Eventually, I discovered that chemicals did an even better job because they helped me to become numb—even numb to the healthy guilt I would have normally felt for doing hurtful things. Addiction helped me disconnect from my moral compass because the pain of the guilt and shame was more than I could bear. It was as if I had an evil librarian inside of me with two card catalogues: one full of shame and one empty of feeling. When I did something I knew was wrong, the librarian added a card to the deep shame catalogue and shut the drawer. I was able to simply toss whatever I couldn't handle under the rug, including my worst deeds, handing it over to the shameful monster I believed I was. He consumed my actions and grew bigger and stronger, as the chemicals helped me distance myself further from my true feelings and my true self.

There may be times as you read this book that you don't like me. That's okay. I didn't like me either. You may become exasperated with me. That's okay, too. I was exasperated with myself, and the people I loved were exasperated with me even more so.

But I hope you'll stay with the story until the end when, after all the twists and turns of this rollercoaster ride I called my life, I finally found a new way to be. I'm now picking up the pieces of a shattered jigsaw puzzle of relationships.

I have written this book for several reasons. First is to confront my lies and finally put them behind me. I've written it to acknowledge my past and begin building on the foundation of truth that's required for successful relationships and a successful me.

My hope is that through reading my story, maybe a liar or two like me out there will understand why they shouldn't live with lies. Maybe they'll finally get that there's so much more potential for living based on their own truth.

I hope that people who are living with sexual trauma will find a place to openly talk about how their experience has affected them. For me, what I went through made it harder to express how I felt about other boys. For others, it might be feelings of guilt about any sexual feelings at all. I hope that we can begin to create more safe environments where it's okay for people to say, "This is what I like and how I feel. It makes me feel wrong and dirty." And I hope that the listeners in those environments will envelop the speakers with love and show them that they aren't bad or wrong because of what they experienced or because of who they are.

Most importantly, I've written this so that my two darling sons never feel they have to lie like I did to themselves, to me, or to their family and friends.

The truth, just like sobriety, is a one-day-at-a-time kind of deal, and I'm well aware that I'm still a work in progress.

I suppose it's my most fervent hope that these pages will demonstrate that regardless of what you've done or where you are in your life, you can begin to live free of that weight on your shoulders. You can learn to live a life filled with light and love.

Note: Some names have been changed to protect the privacy of those involved. Those who may be triggered should be aware that there are stories of trauma in this book, including sexual assault and abuse, suicide, and the tragic thought processes of an addict.

ONE

MINNIE MOUSE

Donald Duck's hand felt huge on my six-year-old back, as the photo of the two of us was snapped. The country bears sang their tunes and bounced around the theater—just like the teddy bears in my house that I dreamt came alive as I slept. And when we entered the Magic Castle, I felt like my family and I turned into royals, just like the kings and queens I'd seen in movies.

Most of the costumed characters scared me when they came close, and I was too small for the majority of the rides. But like a lot of kids, Disney World ignited my innocent imagination

The castles, characters, rides, sweets, bright colors, and piercing noises of laughter and fun are a feast for the senses for both children and adults. Formative memories are bound to be made, whether good or bad. My mother says I was never the same after that trip, and I agree.

She blamed the change in me on a ride called the Human Body. Since it wasn't really a ride, I was allowed to experience it. We all filed into the seats, following the family in front of us. It felt like we were sitting in a little movie theater, except it didn't smell like popcorn, just plastic and water.

I asked my mom why it smelled damp, and that's when I learned what four-dimensional means. This movie shot water at you! I was pretty excited to discover this. After securing ourselves in the seats, the large screen showed a big human mouth opened wide, and we slowly approached it. I began feeling anxious, as it felt like we were a submarine sandwich about to be eaten by a giant. But the narrator calmly explained what was going to happen: "Today, we will start our journey of the human body by entering the mouth."

The big screen got closer and closer, and the chair holding me seemed to grow larger. The group of ten or so people around me disappeared as I became totally immersed in the big screen.

"Then, we will fly into the digestive system and cruise on into the bloodstream, just like food would do," the narrator continued. "Hold on tight; here we go!"

Suddenly, the chairs lunged forward in a tilt, making it feel as though I was going to blast forward toward the screen and smash into it like a gnat. After flying through the throat, we dropped into the stomach, our chairs bellowed back, and I heard a loud splashing sound. It felt like we were swishing around like food in a gurgling pool of stomach acid. My tummy turned, and like a nursing baby, I reached over for the touch of my mother, only to find that the straps around me were too tight. While they ensured one form of security, they prevented the form I desperately needed.

"Next, we'll go into the small intestine, where we will be taken up by the bloodstream," said the narrator, enthusiastically.

A splash of water hit my face as we moved into the small intestine, and my body went into complete catatonic surprise.

The ride seemed so real and the visuals so lifelike that by the time it was done, I was wide-eyed, overwhelmed, speechless, and in tears.

After seeing my reaction, I suppose it makes sense that my mother would blame the sudden difference in me on this ride. But something far more incipient and undetected was at work inside my little mind.

During the time we walked through those hallowed grounds, we saw every Disney character imaginable. But it wasn't Mickey Mouse, with his silly gestures, mouse tuxedo, and high-pitched voice who captured my imagination. I was most intrigued by Minnie Mouse with her adorable polka dot dress and white frilly underwear that tufted out with every step and delicate swirl of her body.

Then, when it came time to leave Disney World—before strolling out through the big blue and white gates into the dreaded, expansive, and hot parking lot for our long drive back to Atlanta—we were gifted with a huge surprise: *a trip inside the souvenir shop!* My brother and I had asked every time we passed by the shop. "Can we, can we, can we go in, *please?*"

Our parents responded with, "Not now. We have more rides to do!" Their distraction tactics worked temporarily, as we turned our attentions away from the store.

But when we finally got to go inside, boy-oh-boy was it worth the wait! There were toys, Legos, candy, and even blankets so that you could wrap your bed up with Disney World and never leave it, even when you fell asleep. There were posters, cups, shirts, hats, and even costumes so that you could become your favorite character at home. But best of all, every Disney character was filled with stuffing and just waiting to be taken home as a new best friend. Before letting us loose, my father said, "All right, boys, you have thirty minutes to pick out your favorite souvenir, but you only get *one thing*."

Well, it didn't take me that long. Within a couple of strides, I was in the Minnie Mouse section. All I had to narrow down was which dress I liked the best. About five minutes later, I walked up to my dad from behind, my head about even with his waist. I grabbed his hand, he turned his strong shoulders, and he tilted his torso down to look at me. "I found the souvenir I want!"

My mother came out from around the corner where she had been looking at snow globes. I held up the stuffed character I was so proud of—the one I related to the most. My new best friend.

My dad straightened his torso, and my mom stood up erect as they looked at each other and laughed.

In that instant, I became flushed, hot, and confused. Why were they laughing? At the same time, my brother Benjamin frolicked over with Goofy, all lanky and wobbly. When he saw Minnie Mouse in my hands, he laughed, too.

"Mark, you can't get Minnie Mouse! You're a boy!" he said.

Seeing her baby cower in shame and confusion, my mother said, "Oh, hush!" She crouched down in sympathy and put her arm around me. "Mark, you sure can have Minnie, but can you tell me why you chose her and not Mickey?"

I didn't know what to say. "I guess I just like her frilly white underwear," I answered timidly. They all giggled, and I felt even more ashamed.

I couldn't figure out why they laughed at me or why it was wrong to feel like I did.

TWO

THE BEAUTY FORT

It was Saturday with the extended family—a perfectly normal day. Nothing special.

As I walked in the front door with Benjamin, we were surprised by Cody, who came swinging around the corner from the stairwell that was hidden from view. He had a big smile on his face, which meant he must have been doing something great downstairs—usually either watching a football game, playing an intense video game, or gearing up for hide-and-seek. This particular day, he said, "Come check out the huge fort I made!"

The expansive fort was constructed of all the spare linens in the house and stretched the surface area of the basement. Underneath was a heaping pile of fresh laundry serving as our congregation spot when my brother and I crawled underneath.

"Let's have a beauty contest!" Cody suggested.

"How are we going to have a beauty contest?" Benjamin asked. "We're all boys, and boys don't have beauty contests."

We all looked at each other, anticipating who would be the

first to come up with a solution. I personally liked the idea, but I had no idea how it was supposed to be conducted.

"We'll get Mark to try on my sister's underwear and rate him!" Cody explained in an "aha moment" with a big smile on his awkward prepubescent face.

A funny feeling developed in my stomach, and I knew something wasn't quite right. I didn't much like being in my underwear in front of other people. I knew for certain I wouldn't like being in someone else's underwear in front of other people—particularly a girl's underwear…and in front of my brother!

"Okay, I guess I'll be a judge," Benjamin sheepishly agreed.

Underneath the blanket, my heart began to throb wildly. I was excited, but I was also unsure about it all. After all, it had only been a week since my family had made fun of me for liking Minnie Mouse's underwear.

As the two older boys left the confines of our blanket mansion so that I could change, I worried that I would be laughed at again.

"I don't really want to do this, guys," I forced out under my breath, lips pursed.

"It's okay, Mark. We're just playing around!" I heard through the blankets that were loosely draped overhead. "We won't tell anyone," Cody said.

But then, Benjamin appeared to become uncomfortable. "I think I'm going to go upstairs," he told Cody. Maybe he was trying not to appear like a spoil sport when he added, "Tell me if he does it, and I'll have the final say on the rating."

As I heard Benjamin's footsteps ascend the stairs, muffled by the carpet, my heart sank. He was two-and-a-half years older than me, and I looked up to him. He had always protected me, and I knew if we were truly doing something wrong, he would stop me. At least this is what went through my mind as he left me behind in the musty basement.

But I went ahead and pulled my pants down. Then, I slid a pair of panties up over my cold little legs. I looked down and felt wiggly, so I wiggled. I popped out of the fort and danced around, laughing like I was performing. Then, I dove back under the blankets and heard Cody laugh.

"Oh, my God, he did it!" Cody yelled up the stairs to where my brother had escaped. "Come watch, Benjamin. It's hilarious!"

I was already changing out of the first costume and into the next pair of lace, when I heard Benjamin say, "No, I think I'm going to stay up here. I don't think this is what we're supposed to be doing."

Hearing that from my older brother made me a little anxious. Through Cody's laughter and my bounding heart rate, my six-year-old brain began to quickly sort through what little I knew about morality, sexuality, and gender roles. But I had no luck making sense of what was happening. All I knew was it was fun. It was funny. So I popped out of the blanket fort again, this time with a smile, and was again met with laughter.

Back within the safety of the fort, I tried to catch my breath. Light pierced the maroon blanket, bathing my naked body in blood red as I peered down, examining my torso, legs, and toes. "Is this wrong?" I asked myself. I had no answer.

Just then, Cody piped up, "Okay, now do it without the underwear!"

Fueled by momentum, I shouted, "Okay! When should I come out?"

Then came the countdown: "3, 2, 1—show time!"

11

I busted out like a dog leaping from the bathtub, loose and unleashed. In a flash of flesh, I tore across the basement for less than ten seconds before diving back into the blanket fortress.

Cody poked his head in and laughed, "Ha ha! That was great!"

I felt a sense of accomplishment. As the youngest boy of fourteen cousins (two of whom were girls and twelve of whom were scattered somewhere between boy and manhood), I longed for the relief, satisfaction, and acceptance that came when I drew laughter. At that young age, I would have done anything to feel accepted by the older heroes in my life. But my reaction to the laughter was mixed. On the one hand, it made me feel worthy and cool. On the other hand, it made me feel anything but accepted. I couldn't quite figure out if they were laughing *with* me or *at* me.

"Now, we're behind the scenes," Cody whispered in a smug, "director" sort of way.

I knew at this point that Benjamin wasn't coming back downstairs. He wasn't the type, and still isn't, to change his mind once it's been made. I was alone with Cody under the fort, and I was naked.

"Do you know what sex is, Mark?"

"Isn't that what God told us not to do until we get married?"

"No, no. I saw my brother and his girlfriend doing it in the shower," he said. "We're supposed to practice before we get married. We just aren't supposed to make babies."

It made sense to me, so I nodded my head, covering my privates with my hands under the warm red glow of the lights shining through the plaid blanket-fort ceiling.

"Why don't you be the girl from the beauty contest? I'll be the boy behind the scenes, and we can practice, too?" he asked in an innocent tone.

"Okay," I answered. "What do I do?"

Unlike so many other childhood memories, what happened next is still as vivid for me today as if it happened yesterday. In a bewildering flash, I learned about gender roles, morality, and sex—or at least to the best of my understanding at six years old. I learned exactly how a girl is supposed to act in a "behind the scenes with a boy" scenario. That led me to see myself primarily as a sex object. Sadly, it also caused me to view women primarily as sex objects.

As soon as Cody had finished with me, I quickly searched for Benjamin. I needed my brother's validation and protection. I needed to feel a sense of hope—anything to lift me out of my moral confusion.

I found Benjamin in the kitchen and walked over to him until I was standing close enough to whisper. He was only two-and-a-half years older than me, but I trusted him to answer my question. I was still a head-and-a-half shorter, so I looked up at him and asked quietly, "Is sex a bad thing?"

He didn't take long to react and answer.

"Well, God forbids it . . . and you can get AIDS like Magic Johnson," he said with his head held in the typical cocksureness of an older sibling.

Guilt, shame, and fear began to boil in my blood, coursing through my vessels and sticking in my brain like plaque. There was my definitive answer, but the confusion swirling around was immense—too much for my young mind to process. I just know that for most of my life, this experience would cloud my ability to make clear-headed and open-hearted decisions free from those ugly emotions that poisoned me after hearing my brother's words.

Suddenly, I felt humiliated about something I'd been told to do by someone I trusted. To further complicate the matter, I had liked it . . . but clearly, I wasn't supposed to.

I wasn't supposed to like Minnie Mouse either. But I began to realize why I liked her frilly white underwear. I wanted boys to look at me like Mickey looked at Minnie. I wanted them to think I was cute like her, and I wanted them to be curious about what might be underneath that underwear.

But I was wrong to like her, and I was wrong to like boys. I was wrong to enjoy acting like a girl with Cody, and I was dirty because I might have gotten AIDS. I was also convinced that no matter what I did, other guys would laugh at me. I desperately needed their approval, but for a long time, I never felt accepted by other boys or men.

These events with Minnie Mouse and Cody were the hallmark episodes in my young life that set the stage for years of torment and a theater of lies.

THREE

THE FIRST LIE

After my experience with Cody, my mind was swimming with the immorality of sex, God's vengeance, AIDS, and why Magic Johnson had it. *Was I going to hell? Did I have AIDS? Was I meant to be a girl?* I couldn't shake these thoughts, and I was desperate to find out what they were all about.

My senses became hypersensitive. Small noises caused me to flinch. I was as reactive as an electrical current. When my brother walked by me, I would cower as though he were going to hit me, even though he was never a mean brother at all.

I looked to confide in the one person with whom I'd found the most peace, love, acceptance, and trust. From my mother flowed my comfort, my affirmations, and my relief—like a fresh spring to an arid life.

"If only I knew what to ask her," I thought as our minivan bounced up and down the 500-mile stretch of concrete highway between Atlanta, Georgia and our beach house. *Thump thump. Thump thump. Thump thump.* I contemplated how to come forth with the dreadfully difficult news.

Finally, the steam reached the lid, my anxiety made my face hot, and my stomach turned, as I blurted out, "Mom?" with a worried tone, like I had just seen a crime take place on the street.

She glanced over to me quickly, while somehow talking smoothly and slowly. Her movements and mannerisms were always so controlled, so majestic, light and beautifully orchestrated with such poise that it was like watching a ballet.

"What is it, my dear?"

A long, uneasy pause followed. I slumped down into the front seat of the car. (This was before it was illegal for a six-year-old to ride in the front.) I debated with myself. *Do I tell her? Well, it's kind of too late not to tell her.*

I couldn't think of anything to say but what had been burning a hole through my skull. So it just came bubbling out: "How do you get AIDS?"

Crap. The cat was out of the bag. My mom knew everything. When my brother and I misbehaved in the back seat of the car, she'd say things like, "You know, boys, I have eyes in the back of my head." I believed her. She seemed to always catch anything uncouth before injury or poor manners occurred. I had reason to believe that in just asking a question like this, I was totally transparent. In my mind, she must already know that I had sex done to me. My fear continued to bubble.

"AIDS?" she suddenly smirked a little bit, giving me an ever-so-slight tinge of relief. But I knew such questions could ultimately bring out something I wasn't entirely ready to share.

AIDS was still new and just becoming a very popular topic around Atlanta. Magic Johnson had just retired from professional basketball because of it, and from what I'd heard, some crazy people were putting it on fuel pump handles, trying to spread the disease.

My mother avoided the question, not necessarily because she was uncomfortable with the topic, but because she wanted someone to blame for her little boy's fear. "Is this because of that damn TV?" She liked to blame the media, movies, or anything secular for any of our childhood anxieties.

"No, Mom," I hissed back.

"Then, why does someone your age need to know?"

The world around me seemed to sharpen and close in, and the sound of our minivan's engine became a distant echo as fearful thoughts took residence in place of actual experience. My brain felt as though it was slowly swelling up, and I felt dizzy and more than a little squeamish. Memories from the basement beauty pageant played out in my head, paralyzing me and making me feel cold and lonely.

I no longer felt comfortable and secure around my mother. I had lost her as a safety net. I was on my own, curiously and fearfully speechless.

I had never been so alone, but I knew rather quickly that this was a solace to me—a new home, a new form of freedom that would keep me safe. My mind calmed down as a little lie came to me and slid from my lips, innocently cutting through time and becoming a new habit: *My First Lie.*

"I'm just wondering how someone like Magic Johnson got AIDS," I said.

"Oh, son, if you do as God says and only have sex with the woman you marry, you don't have to worry about diseases like AIDS."

The conversation was over, but my fear had just begun. The lingering, confusing dread continued to stink up my mind like a broken, rotting egg. *I have AIDS, I can't even trust my mother to help me, I'm clearly going to hell, and I'm pretty sure I'd like being a girl better than a boy.*

These deep-rooted beliefs festered inside me. I was afraid of who I had become (even though I was only just becoming anything), afraid of intimacy and trusting others (even though intimacy was readily available), and afraid of trusting a God who was apparently out to get me and send me to hell.

These three fears would become the wheels under the carriage of my life.

FOUR

FAMILY

I was still in the crib when my family moved from our house that backed up to the Chattahoochee River in Atlanta. Yet, strangely, I can still remember everything from the arrangement of furniture in my nursery to the soft linen around my mother's bosom where I rested my face as she carried me crying from the crib to the nearby rocking chair.

It was a two-story house with a two-car garage and a huge yard. The lawn had big, wiry, willow-like bushes with rough, long-hanging tendrils that could cut soft little fingers if you weren't careful. The bushes looked as if they were characters out of Jim Henson's *Fraggle Rock* TV series. If I had been old enough to be outside alone at night, I wouldn't have dared walk past them. Even from the safe confines of my car seat, they scared me as we pulled past them into our driveway. I imagined that trolls inhabited those hanging bushes of gloom and could turn a kid into stone.

The house had a big glass door with fancy sand-stroke contours that looked like a scene Bob Ross would paint, but without color. One day, I hit it with a little toy hammer. I felt a sense of accomplishment when the landscape shattered into a million pieces. I still vividly remember the thunder of pain as I winced from the subsequent spanking. I tried to run, but my butt was too sore to support such strides. My dad shed tears when he hugged me afterwards.

My mother's embrace was warm as she cradled me in the rocking chair. I can recall her nursing gown and the position of the chair in the corner of the room, facing the crib where I had been rescued. The pale light seeped through the curtains, keeping me quiet but awake, as I listened to my mother hum and breathed in her love.

Despite my belief after my AIDS question that I could no longer count on my mom, my family was solid as a rock. I didn't come from a hard life of adversity and challenge, and family conflict. This even applies to my extended family. I count many of them among my best friends, and they care deeply about me.

My mother has such deep roots of love, compassion, nourishment, and health that her mere presence makes me shake in my shame-filled boots. She has always encouraged me with a spark that exposes my darkness and makes me see the light inside me. She repeatedly told me how wonderfully gifted, talented, and blessed I was, and when she was around, I began to believe I was worthy. But when she wasn't around, I fell prey to my shame again.

My father Ben is a value driven man you cannot budge. Not fire nor wind, light nor dark, heaven nor hell will stop him from standing firm. He is as consistent as a sundial in the desert.

I've been told that twenty years before I was born, he still had some growing up to do. Like a seasoned gardener, however, he noticed the toxic behaviors restricting the growth of his family and not only pulled away the weeds, but found the root cause and the remedy. He powered through mediocre self-help books and found that he connected most with the Bible. He never turned back, and thus created a world in which even the sky didn't seem to be a limit. For him, the sky became the starting point as he reached toward the heavens, grabbed hold of the swinging gates, and pulled his family and business with him.

Now, he leads a successful engineering firm that he built from the ground up, he's healthy in his seventies, and everyone in my family looks up to him. I don't think anyone besides my mother could say anything negative about him, and that's just because she knows him better than anyone else. Plus, of course, no one is perfect. Whatever she knows, she holds it all so close to her loving heart that the devil himself couldn't pull it out and wield it as a weapon.

My older sisters saw our family go from struggling paupers to fair kings as my dad worked hard for his success. By the time my brother and I were born, the American Dream seemed a reward well fought for.

So unlike my sisters, I never experienced financial depravity or the emotional unavailability of an absent father.

Then, there's my brother, who has integrity that emulates my father's. Melody Beattie wrote that the first step to rejecting shame is accepting who we are. That's Benjamin. It isn't that he rejects shame, but he accepts who he is and sports it proudly. From a young age, he seemed so sure of himself—to the point of annoyance. Like my father, he has always been a strong role model in my life. I wanted to be more like them—more certain of who I was and happier with who I had been and who I was becoming.

Benjamin is now successful and shows love to his wife and two sons with an authenticity I wish I could emulate. When he says, "I love you," he really means it. He may not be perfect, but at least he doesn't fake it…and probably couldn't fake it if he tried. My mother says he was always the worst liar.

Legend has it that as a child, when asked if he had done something he wasn't supposed to do, he couldn't help but roll his eyes into the back of his head, exposing the whites of his eyes like a zombie caught in a headlight. My theory is that this reflex was such a dead giveaway that he just stopped lying altogether.

In contrast, I struggled to accept who I was. I was too scared to let go and too scared of the repercussions. Unfortunately, you can't reject shame if you can't accept who you are.

Both of our sisters say my brother and I lived different lives.

Speaking of my sisters, who are both more than twenty years older, they represent love in the way they mother their families. I don't know how our parents had two sets of kids so far apart. This is a huge testament to their love for each other. These two American Christian lovers make Romeo and Juliet seem lame. While Shakespeare's lovers gave up and accepted death, my parents fought hard for their lives and their love. Giving up wasn't in their vocabulary, and their great love expanded to their four children, eleven grandchildren, and two great-grandchildren.

If I could change one thing about my family, though, I guess it would be their tendency to brush issues under the carpet. This trait had two effects on me. For bad behaviors, a consequence would come, and after that, the topic would rarely be discussed again. This allowed little opportunity for reflection and little room for individual and relational growth. I also felt that it was my responsibility to keep secrets. It was my job to hide my fears, mask my guilt, and never disclose my weaknesses. It was my job to hide the truth about myself.

FIVE

SEA ISLAND & NEW FEARS

S hortly before I turned five years old, a year before my sexual confusion and shame began, my family packed up and moved to Sea Island. Despite my many memories from infancy, I remember little about this move. I only recall sitting on some boxes in the back of the moving truck, feeling like the king of the world. This was about a year before the sexual confusion began.

The moving truck left a busy city where the neighborhood sidewalk was unsafe for tricycle riding. It then parked itself on an island oasis where ocean spray flavored every day, and the sound of rolling waves carried my mind through long childhood nights.

Sea Island is a magical land with colonial ruins jutting out of the ground in peculiar spaces, with historians speculating about the roles of each structure. Modern, colossal buildings befitting a royal family are erected all over the island. Inside these grandiose, lavish castles are people dressed as butlers, who even say "sir" to little boys and "ma'am" to little girls. They serve every whim with a smile and place cookies and mints beside every door like fairies.

Sea Island is quite literally the safest place on earth that I know. Benjamin and I used to knock on an old service door hidden behind a swampy turtle pond, and an old African American man would pop out with a plate full of cookies.

"Two's all you boys get, or your mamma'll have my heinie," he'd say, while we wrestled with the impossible decision of choosing between cinnamon raisin, chocolate chip, macadamia nut, double-chocolate truffle, and more. By some miracle, no matter what time of day it was, they were always hot. We painstakingly selected our two and dashed back to the pond where we continued catching turtles and frogs. We never thought twice about our privilege and freedom while the marshy salt water on our hands mixed with the chocolate chips and sugar in our mouths.

This place was a big change from where we started and where my sisters were raised. Never in the history of Atlanta has it been safe for two young boys to go knocking on hidden service doors. If we had done that in the city, we would have received spankings comparable to the thrashings in a Roman torture chamber.

But in a place like Sea Island, where acceptance seeped through every crack, it's a wonder that a boy like myself would grow up with so much fear that he couldn't accept the love and acceptance of family or friends. And that he would abstain from intimacy as if it were the plague.

Other than sharks, there wasn't much to fear on this island of ruins and castles…except one neighborhood house. It was cloaked in Spanish moss, and disheveled ivy draped over the trusses, blocking each doorway from sight. The house was mysterious, and my imagination, left unattended, led me to some horrific fantasies.

It was sharks, however, that became my first fear for which I developed a coping strategy. One Friday night after dinner, we sat down as a family in front of the large box TV that had a console the size of a refrigerator.

My father walked into the living room in his tiny yellow shorts, eighties tank top, and an overflowing bowl of popcorn. My mother sat next to me, legs crossed in her soft white nightgown. My brother sat straight up, hair poking up on his crown and grinning mischievously through his missing two front teeth.

"It's gonna be scary, baby Mark!" he said.

I sat curled up next to my mother, contained and well-behaved, as my father popped in the VHS tape titled *JAWS*, its blood-red capital letters printed boldly across the plastic cover. So as not to ruin anything, we had to close our eyes as the tape rewound.

It was a fact of the nineties that no rental movie ever came ready to watch. In the days of VHS, movie-viewing involved a tedious wait time as the VCR (the device that played the VHS tape) made a noise like it was eating the movie with small grinding gears returning the tape to the beginning. For this movie, it only increased the anticipation and the ultimate impact of what we were about to witness.

While some children may not have found *JAWS* to be traumatic, shrugging off the images much like you'd flick a fly off of your food, my experience was vastly different. I was the kid who couldn't walk down a dark hallway alone. My mother used to walk me to the bathroom from the dinner table, and since she'd leave while I was in there, I would run the entire way back with the hair on the back of my neck sticking up like a cat's fur.

After seeing an image of Medusa, the Greek goddess with snakes slithering out of her head, I developed a fear that snakes would come out of the toilet. Therefore, I would sprint back to the dinner table as if I was running from the head of Medusa, who was rising from the depths of the septic system to turn me to stone.

Still, I was coming to view our Sea Island home as mostly a comfortable, safe world. That view came crashing spectacularly down, and my fear reached an entirely new level when I witnessed the sheer brutality of sharks in *JAWS*. This shark not only swallowed men whole, but it bit through ships. I'd previously thought the only way a ship could sink was with a torpedo or a tidal wave. The tiny boy-mind that thought Medusa was going to materialize out of the toilet began sitting up at night, fearful that a shark would launch out of the ocean and crash his bloodthirsty face through my window to devour me, my family, *and* our house.

Fears such as *JAWS* and Medusa are what the professionals call "irrational," but this young boy believed his fears were entirely rational.

I became preoccupied, making sleep a difficult task. I hid the fear inside, though, and within a week or two, I began experimenting with various cures.

My first coping mechanism involved obsessive compulsive disorder-type (OCD) behaviors. I would lie awake, wrestling with images of the *JAWS* shark and that horrifying Medusa. Then, all of a sudden, as if my mind was protecting me, I would get caught in a new thought: "Is the door to our house closed?" It wasn't that I was scared of the door being open. All I know is this thought was so pervasive that it drowned out the horror movie and replaced it with something I could obsess over. I couldn't sleep unless I got up to remedy the situation. So eventually, I would crawl out of bed, slowly tiptoe across the creaky upstairs wood floor of our 1800s-built home, and arrive at the staircase.

While standing at the top of the stairs, I could peer across the fireplace mantle of the living room below and see the comfortable cushions puffed and fluffed, as they cast shadows on the large oriental rug. Beyond the rug was the front door, which, despite my worries, was always closed.

Still, seeing the front door closed was as unsatisfactory as a person of authority saying about a moral dilemma, "because God said so." I needed a better confirmation than sight. I had to feel, touch, and hear the door latch to believe we were truly safe.

I felt ashamed and confused by my actions, which is why I carefully crept down the steps like a bank robber. I leapt over the last two steps, as they were particularly creaky and could easily awaken my mother. Had she come out to console me, dressed in her bathrobe as a mother might do when their child has a nightmare, there would be no way to soothe me. I was no longer in fear. Checking the door calmed me down, so if she had hugged me, I would have simply stood there, feeling unsatisfied by her efforts. Had I rendered my mother's love obsolete?

This OCD self-soothing of my fear manifested itself on countless nights until it got worse and became increasingly more difficult to manage. I would lie awake and wait until I didn't hear anyone stirring around the house. When all was quiet, I would sneak downstairs and open and close the front, back, side, and porch doors. Then, I would check the linen and game closet doors, before making my rounds in the kitchen. I would secure each drawer, slowly, so as not to rattle the forks and knives. Then, I'd climb up on the counter to open and close each cabinet door. Before I left the cool, clean, white-tiled kitchen, I would check the refrigerator, followed by the pantry door. Stealthily, I would then make my way back upstairs, where I would finally lie down and exhale, relieved.

One evening, after making my obsessive-compulsive rounds, my anxiety didn't dissipate like most nights. I was confused and had to pee, but I was so stricken by anxiety and fear that I just lay there, eyes wide open. I peered deep through the dark into the ceiling above my head and let that tension go, purposefully wetting my bed in the process. When the wetness turned cold, I took off my clothes and looked down at myself.

Earlier that week in the extended family's basement, I had learned something about my body that no six-year-old should ever be taught. What I had been taught would become a new obsession that was so much more effective than shutting cabinet doors: masturbation.

This new obsession, however, was not acceptable behavior in my family. We were too Christian to play with private parts. So here was something else to add to my shame.

SIX

CHRISTIAN MORNINGS

Every morning, the steam from white plates filled with fresh southern-style, home-cooked breakfast filled our noses. My father would sit Benjamin and me down daily, without fail, and monotonously read one chapter of Proverbs from the Bible. King Solomon, the wisest king in the history of man, wrote Proverbs to impart great wisdom to all future generations of God's people. If you ask me, that's a very tall order!

The reading seemed like steel wool on a chalk board, so like countless other children through time, I resisted each word. I reluctantly pulled my eyes from the biscuits and gravy in front of me so that I could appear to be listening. With thirty-one chapters, Proverbs meant that we never had a day off to eat without first hearing a soul-nourishing appetizer of wisdom.

I'm still amazed at my parents' persistent drive to attend services on Sundays, given the many creative diversions and catastrophic scenarios that two brothers, both resistant to the idea of church, could conjure. But we went, week in and week out, on vacations, holidays, during hurricane season, and on Super Bowl Sunday.

I didn't have any gripe with God or the people there. It was the fear of the person I believed I was that made me not want to be there. As far as my six-year-old self was concerned, I'd already had sex, and that was a sin. Making my situation even worse, I liked it and found ways to replicate that feeling so that it would relieve my anxiety and fear. I believed I deserved hell.

SEVEN

I DON'T FIT IN

My face went hot, and my head felt like a balloon ready to pop.

This was how I always felt when someone around me made a homophobic or any kind of sexual joke. I wanted so much to fit in, but participating in it would have meant ridiculing myself. Whenever this type of talk started, whether in the boy's bathroom or while changing after P.E., I would lower my head, avoid eye contact, and try to get myself out of there as soon as possible. That balloon feeling would continue until class commenced. And I couldn't shed the fear that the other boys would be able to see my silent secret and reveal it to the world.

That fear would remain until I did something about it. That something involved the earth-shattering, reality-breaking, warm flow release of an orgasm ricocheting through my body.

While I was known as a sweet kid with good intentions, coping with challenging life situations became increasingly complex, so I found an additional solution: *mischief*.

One school day in the boys' bathroom, I discovered how to use mischief to completely divert the pressure I was feeling inside. While the boys were playing, joking about queers and stuff, I decided to take shit out of the toilet and smear it all over the wall. The shock of this rippled through the jokesters in the bathroom, immediately prompting a change of subject, as their laughter echoed down the school's hallway.

From then on, I was labeled a "class clown." Ultimately, I was just willing to go to any extreme to achieve a diversion from the clashing inside my soul. Believing that my secrets would be found out led me to do extraordinary things. These actions often hurt others and typically cast me in a negative light that I didn't intend. But I was willing to suffer the consequences as long as my secrets lost their potency.

As time went on, I felt I had to hide more and more. I had a friend whose mother was dead and whose father left copies of *Penthouse* magazine beside the toilet in their house. *Playboy* never did it for me; from a very early age, I only liked porn if there was a guy in it.

One night when we were between six and seven years old, his father, who was messed up in his own ways, left us alone in the house for the evening. We found some of his dad's porn videos and watched them. Afterwards, we invited his younger brother upstairs for a game of Truth or Dare, but there was one rule to join the game: no one was allowed to wear clothes.

We only engaged in the slightest sexual play that was more joking than serious, but it only added to my uncertainty about AIDS. And it extended the depths of the closet where I hid my true self.

Even though no one would know unless we said something, I still felt the urgency to do something drastic to hide the incident. So I crossed an unheard of First Grade boundary.

The elementary school cafeteria was large enough to hold the entire student body. Everyone was enjoying their food and conversations, while I sat there with my head feeling hot and inflated like it did when I became stressed. I was sitting across from a girl named Lauren, who was beautiful and new to the school. I was thrilled to be sitting across from her because I could tell the other boys envied my proximity.

I noticed the boys looking down the long island of cafeteria tables, peering over cardboard juice boxes and plastic Lunchables, their grins suggesting to me that it was time I make a move. I thought if I didn't, I might as well admit I liked boys. So, once the heat inside my little beating heart became unbearable, I looked Lauren dead in the eye. Running out of time to make my mark in terms of First Grade masculinity, I said "hello" in a way that suggested I had much more to say. "Hey, Lauren?"

She paused, as she put down her peanut butter and jelly sandwich and softly wiped her smooth lips. "Uh…yeah?"

"Can I ask you something?" slid out of my quivering lips.

"Uh, sure," she said, looking up and down the table nervously and taking in the thrill of the expectant eyes from my curious classmates. As Lauren blushed, the boys waited in anticipation for my question to come out.

"Will…uh…will…," I stammered. "Will you have sex with me after school?"

"What?!" she gasped as she pushed her hands against the cafeteria table and arched her back. All eyes were on us, as the cafeteria went absolutely silent. No one wanted to miss a moment of this. I had done it again, going as far as possible to shock everyone.

"Did you just ask if I'll have sex with you? I barely know what that means!" she said as she rose from the table, swinging her dress. She turned her body in the direction of the teacher who had the daily duty to keep an eye on us while we ate. She then walked briskly away with long, purposeful strides. The teacher bent down, her hair hanging over their two heads as she prepared to hear what Lauren had thought so imperative to share.

Suddenly, the teacher sprang up and glared at me, her eyes settling deep within her sockets like she wasn't sure what to do.

Laughter came roaring from my friends, but the teacher's footsteps, coming right toward me—the very sound of impending doom—was so ominous that everyone soon hushed. She grabbed me by the collar and dragged me out of the cafeteria. I was whisked away to the principal's office and didn't return to school for a number of days.

But I didn't feel remorse. I felt accomplished. There was no way anyone would even believe it if my secret emerged.

Girls. Why hadn't I thought of girls before? They were the perfect out.

EIGHT

FRIENDS, SPORTS, & THE OLYMPICS

I was certain I didn't want people to find out about me, but I was still uncertain about who I was or who I was becoming. As I started to get older, friendships became important, but I didn't feel I had much to bring to the table. Most kids had something to show off and could talk about how great they were.

Instead, I came to friendship to *take* from the table. I would sort of emulate the person I was attracted to. I became a chameleon, assuming (or attempting to assume) someone else's identity to see if it would fit. I'd check myself in the mirror and take my new persona out into the street to see if I got favorable reactions.

Soon, I looked up to a new kid who moved to Sea Island. I was initially attracted to Michael because he was tall, funny, and could draw a cartoon in less than a minute that would make Walt Disney envious.

One rainy south Georgian day, Michael and I were sitting in his room on huge bean bag chairs. We were watching the

Batman movie in which Danny DeVito played the Penguin. It's an awkward scene when he first appears. At the sight of the character, Michael and I looked at each other and grimaced like there was a rotten egg in the room. Nose up, eyes squinted, and lips drawn back, he relaxed his shoulders and said, "Penguins are my favorite animal, but not that penguin!"

I rolled onto the floor from the bean bag chair and let out a roar of laughter. He joined the giggle fest, and when it subsided, we kept our eyes glued to the TV until the scene was done.

Then, I lied when I said, "Penguins are my favorite animal, too. I love how they walk!"

Honestly, I didn't have a favorite animal, nor had I ever thought about it. But I figured, W*hy not? They're likable, and Michael, the new cool kid, likes them.* I couldn't draw worth a damn, but if I liked penguins, we had something in common to form a bond.

Michael and I actually ended up having a lot in common. He became one of my best friends and later a best man at my wedding. I was always so excited to see him and hear his jokes, watch him draw, and pick up mannerisms that might make me funny, too.

Unfortunately, most of my friendships followed this pattern. I would meet someone whose character I admired, and to better my view of myself, I would emulate him or her. I even had friends who annoyed me, but I stuck around them to vicariously pick up some part of their cool, exciting identity. That way, I could better hide my own identity.

In my entire life, there was only one friendship where this wasn't the case. That was Buster. For this boy, I had a love that I couldn't fully understand because it didn't fit my pattern.

We fed off each other and energized each other. We explored with each other, and we were partners on an adolescent journey. But other than that experience, I was more of a taker than a giver, which breaks my heart since I truly knew some amazing people.

At the same time that my childhood friendships began to develop, I was shown the glory of—and developed a subsequent fascination for—sports. Of course, I knew what sports were. My dad watched games nearly every night, and we frequently went to football, basketball, and baseball games.

My parents tried to keep Benjamin and me involved in a sport every season to boost our confidence, keep us busy, and instill a character of dedication and teamwork. Most of the time, though, I had to be dragged to practice or lured to the stadium as an unwilling spectator. I was only in attendance for the candy, frozen lemonade, or a milkshake.

I was on little league teams where I developed my first crushes, but I was horrible at baseball. There was too much time for my mind to wander to the attractive guys on my own team or the other team. I put on a misleading front by talking about the game and acting excited about the team. But I never really felt a part of the team until I played football.

Both playing and watching football were different for me. Everyone looks the same and does the same thing throughout the game. It's a rather impersonal sport, and I was good at it. After the games, however, I felt just as left out and different as I did with the other sports I played.

My true introduction to sport came in 1996 through a beautiful, spectacular model of human potential: the Olympics.

They fascinated me and allowed me to see athletes as something other than sexual beings.

The marvelous two-week-long event came to Atlanta, and my hometown of five million strangers transformed into a melting pot of athletic observance, respect, and admiration. The city spent in excess of $2 billion on the Olympics, redesigning a baseball stadium into a track and field coliseum of monstrous proportions. They also transformed the entire city from a relic of southern heritage that was burned by General Sherman into a menagerie of athletes and diversity. Of course, they added a splash of character to display our technological advancements and human accomplishments.

Museums popped up, Coca-Cola erected a park to support groundbreaking entertainment, and Six Flags Over Georgia constructed rollercoasters straight out of fantasy. All of this came with a nineties' flair. What a weird, showy time the nineties were. The USA track and field hero of the 1996 Olympic games wore golden running shoes. It wasn't enough to be the fastest human on the planet; you also had to come off as a rock star.

Michael Irvine, a famous wide receiver for the Dallas Cowboys, wore mink coats flashier than Lady Gaga's entire wardrobe. He even wore them to sports interviews. Dennis Rodman tattooed every part of himself, hung huge golden rings from each ear, his lips, and his eyes, and he dressed like a bride for no particular reason. Mike Tyson had a tattoo covering his face, and there was Michael Johnson running in his golden shoes, making each stride seem royal and earth-shattering. Everyone and every institution went above and beyond for the sake of entertainment.

The city of Atlanta was no different, boasting Olympic spirit on every corner. Every bus was repainted with flashy colors. The expansive metro tunnels were filled with mile-long posters of sporting accomplishments with their speedy capsules of inspiration shuttling hundreds of thousands of spectators to and from the stadiums for the big events.

The airport, once a drab gray maze that delivered more confusion and stress than excitement, turned into a museum-like establishment with portraits displaying diversity from every country. Billboards, marquees, blimps, and streamers lit up the city. Atlanta became a quintessential pillar of inspiration. To my young, developing mind, it resembled the legends of ancient Rome. I was in awe.

By the time 1996 rolled around, I had been suspended from school several times. So much was trapped inside of me that I simply didn't know how to control myself within the boundaries of everyday life. I didn't have any other way to deal with my anxiety. My coping strategies were limited to acting out publicly or self-soothing, sexual gratification. So the Olympic pageantry came at the perfect time for me.

I was nine years old and desperately seeking inspiration. I don't remember a great deal from age six to age nine. Those childhood memories are fragmented like a shattered stained glass window shoved into a cylinder. They're a kaleidoscope of poorly pieced-together shards—painful memories of me trying to run from my fears and sexual identity and of hoping to collect new identities in order to mask the shame and learn to cope.

There were nights before attending the Olympics, after my mom put me to bed, where I would stand up after I heard the last thud of her footsteps upon leaving the staircase and slip down my pajamas and little tighty whities. I'd look in the mirror, turn to the side, turn back toward the mirror, and tuck my chin down my short stomach so that my eyes could overlook my undeveloped penis. I would cover it with my hand and imagine what it would be like if it wasn't there. When I pulled my hand back, and the little member shot forward, I'd feel a rush of shame and hide it again. Other times, I held my hand there and considered getting a knife to dismember myself, but I was so scared of blood, having witnessed the human body ride at Disney World, that I'd turn off the lights and masturbate to relieve the tension. I remember thinking of suicide at this time, but I didn't really know what it was. I just thought that maybe I should die since I was born *wrong*.

As I witnessed the Olympics, however, something else began to draw my attention away from my developing body. The events inspired a fascination within me that allowed me to redirect some of my childhood fears into healthy behaviors. The ambition, confidence, and goal-directed discipline of sport helped me greatly for a few years.

I heard stories about impressive Olympic athletes like Wilma Rudolph. An African American born premature to a poverty-stricken family of twenty-one children, she suffered from polio as a child, which paralyzed her, and wore leg braces until she was nine. She overcame this crippling disease, learned to run, and took three gold track and field medals in the 1960 Olympics!

Another athlete, skater Scott Hamilton, was diagnosed with cystic fibrosis at a young age, only to become an ice skating superstar. Then, there was the great Jesse Owens, an African

American man who had the guts to run the 1936 Olympic track in the middle of Nazi Germany! While everyone in the stands looked down on him for being a "lesser human being," he took the gold medal, showing them that he was not their equal—he was better.

Each event had some tear-jerking story attached to it that moved through my heart more intensely than burning a finger in a fire. I was hooked. If these people could do it, maybe I could do something great, too.

I would have done nearly anything to become a professional athlete, so I became highly competitive in extracurricular activities. I had to perform the best, whether it was soccer or four-square. I adopted the Olympic mentality that if I wasn't the best, I was going to be the hardest working. And I succeeded.

While I developed this new jock identity, however, bad habits still died hard. On the one hand, I played every sport—basketball, soccer, American football, and baseball—and I began playing each pretty well. On the other hand, I acted out in class and began pushing the sexual envelope with every girl I knew. At this point, my sports identity was an outlet. In addition, girls were becoming attracted to me, and I could easily divert their gay-dar by being sexual with them. It worked in First Grade, so it would surely continue to work.

I was so competitive, in fact, that it hid the rainbow in my heart. In every sport, I beat the boys I had crushes on. If they were better, I worked harder and came out on top. Sports became a primal scrap to come off as alpha. The feeling of superiority I would momentarily achieve obscured my conflicting identity, while girls became a conquest—a medal of honor that proved my masculinity.

NINE

RAPED

By twelve years old, things were beginning to go somewhat smoothly…until my family took a New Year's vacation to Cancun, Mexico.

My fifteen-year-old brother and I shared a luxury hotel room on the trip. It was out of character for our parents to give us so much free rein. Our room was spectacular, and the resort was lavish with extravagant food, wine, and music.

After we had been there for about three days, just enough time to become familiar with the property and even some of the guests, Benjamin became interested in a beautiful twenty-five-year-old Asian woman. He had met her while shooting pool alone. I was shocked that my teenage brother had picked up such a beautiful, fully grown, and mature woman. Sexuality radiated from her like pixie dust.

One night, she invited Benjamin to meet her on the beach to hang out with a group of older kids. I was too tired, so I stayed in bed, wearing a bathrobe and boxers while watching *Lethal Weapon*. Then, I heard a knock on the door. I thought it must be room service making a mistake or my mom checking on me.

There was a hot tub in the middle of the huge room, and I felt like a prince as I languidly strolled toward the peephole. The Asian woman was standing there. She wore tight, shiny black pants that looked like leather, high heels, and a bikini top. She had a blue streak in her hair that fell across one eye, accentuating her dark complexion. She looked like a gift from heaven, and I was in total shock at her presence at my door.

I opened the door a crack and said, "I thought you were with my brother down at the beach party?"

"Yeah, I was down there, but you weren't. So I came to try and find you. Your brother gave me your room number to come get you."

I opened the door more fully, but still not enough to allow her to enter.

"I didn't want to go. I'm tired."

I was in my underwear and still struggled greatly with inferiority and self-esteem, especially while mostly naked.

"Why did you come to find me?"

"Because," she giggled, continuing in a seductive voice, "I thought you were too cute when we met earlier, and after hanging out with the other boys at the beach, I just wanted to see you tonight."

I felt a warmth come over me. Receiving a compliment like that did something to me that I'd never experienced. She was older, and she was a girl. I felt like a stud muffin the moment the words left her mouth. This feeling of validation from girls would stay with me for many years to come.

"Can I come in?" she asked in a quieter, more approachable voice.

"Uh ... sure, but I'm just in my underwear."

"Perfect," she said as I opened the door fully.

Perfect?! What is going on? I asked myself. My stomach received a bucket of butterflies at the very suggestion.

Not knowing what to do next, I asked, "Do you want to watch *Lethal Weapon*?"

I jumped up on the bed and assumed my previous spot. Then, I pulled the blankets over me to hide my little body. She walked around the foot of the bed slowly and approached the other side, put her hands down, and began crawling toward me. Next, she said something that would leave me shocked and helpless: "I want to teach you how to have sex."

Moments later, she had straddled me and was holding me tightly inside of her. I gazed up toward the blue streak in her hair as it danced across her face and closed eyes. I watched her move like a dancer—so smooth. Her head tilted back, and her lips puckered, suggesting that she was enjoying herself. The motion on top of me was something new, and I remember thinking that it felt rather unremarkable and anticlimactic.

Then, her graceful movements slowed down, and she pushed herself off of me, falling gently onto the down comforter beside me.

I looked at her with shocked and confused eyes. "It's okay. The first time can be scary," she said.

I didn't know what she was talking about.

"Some guys I know can't stay hard, usually because they've been drinking," she continued.

"I'm not drunk," I said.

"Oh—then, let me try this," she said as she put her head under the covers. Feeling her hair slowly drag down my stomach made me feel slightly aroused. Then, she took me in her mouth, rendering me truly helpless.

"This is the best feeling ever," I told her as my eyes rolled back.

She didn't stay down there for long, unfortunately, before she hopped back up to straddle me like before.

But that caused me to lose interest again.

"What can I do?" she asked with a sense of hopelessness.

"I don't know," I answered. "But it's okay. Let's just watch the movie."

She was already off the bed by the time I'd finished answering the question.

"I'd better get back down to the beach, but now that you know what to do, have fun!" she said, smiling.

Coming home after that vacation took some adjusting. I wanted to wear the sexual contact with this woman as a medal, but I felt horrible. First, I didn't even like it, so when I told my friends about it, I had to fake how much fun I'd had. Second, I felt shame because I lost my erection, and I knew that wasn't supposed to happen when you lost your virginity.

I knew the problem: I wanted her to be another boy, not a twenty-five-year-old woman. Losing my virginity wasn't glorious, it wasn't the way I wanted it, and it wasn't the way God intended it to happen for me.

TEN

DRUGS TO THE RESCUE

After age twelve, hormones began rushing in, and all the little things became monumental. Who among us is ever ready for the intensity of those feelings?

Not only was I fluctuating through hormones, I was fluctuating through identities. And I wasn't measuring up to the boy I was hoping to be. I couldn't even perform sexually. When we fail at who we dream of becoming, it's more difficult than failing at who we are. Failing at who we are just requires getting back up. Failing at who we want to be requires a whole new assessment of life.

Straightness, for instance, came natural to most of my friends. But I had to work hard at it. And when things happened in my social life, like getting dumped in a relationship, I felt as if I'd lost everything. Then, I became suicidal. Those thoughts became an obsession and would linger for years.

One day, I decided to go through with my suicidal thoughts. A friend of mine had recently been found hanging in his closet, and that started to sound like a good idea to me. So I tied a rope, but I was unable to find a chair to stand on other than the ones in the kitchen where my mother was making dinner. So the plan would have to wait.

What would I do to waste time until I could see it through? Waiting for a planned death is nauseating. I couldn't bear the anxiety. Then, a thought came into my head.

Earlier that week, I had found a bag of pot on the ground at a nearby soccer field and hid it in my dresser. I didn't really know what to do with it, and I was kind of scared to try it. But being stuck between two fears—death and drugs—I decided to take the one of least impact for the time being.

In order to occupy my mind before hanging myself, I crept into Benjamin's room while he was in the shower. A year earlier, we had made a family trip to Jamaica, and he had purchased a hand-carved trinket pipe. He bought it as a joke, and we laughed for days at the little thing. It was a statue of a Jamaican dude with dreads, sitting Indian style. Buried in his braids was a place to pack the substance to be burned, and between his crossed legs rose a long, dark shaft topped with a mushroom tip and a hole. You would place your lips on his cock and inhale through it. Horribly suggestive!

I went on a long walk with the cock pipe and the bag of weed, hiding deep in the woods. With sweaty palms from anxiety, I struggled with the lighter. Once lit, I puffed until I couldn't bear the intense coughing. Strangely, I didn't feel anything. There was no high, but the thrill was still intense. Somehow, it satiated my desire to die swinging in my closet.

I knew I needed to find a ritual to mask and overpower the smell of smoked pot that had filled my lungs, hair, hands, and mind. So I took off for an hour of walking around, smearing my hands in dirt, leaves, and creek water. I moseyed home for dinner with the family, and immediately after, I left for the woods again with my Jamaican cock man and the rest of the weed.

This time, though, it was different: I got really fucking high. I had found an answer to all of my troubles! I had been graced with a new release, and along with it, a new identity—one that I could wear proudly with my peers and still fit in.

ELEVEN

Shot-gunned Oblivion

"It helps you dance!" my cousin said, almost as if he thought I needed persuading. He was offering me a beer.

"Where are we going to drink?" I asked. "And won't people smell it?"

"Baby Mark, no one will even know we're gone." Even though I was thirteen, Baby Mark was still what everyone called me to separate me from an older cousin they called "Big Mark."

"Look at everyone in this place," my cousin continued. "They're all drinking, so they won't be able to smell it on us!"

We were at my older sister's wedding on Sea Island. I had been petrified in anticipation of the event because the entire family would arrive. I always felt anxious around my extended family. I thought they could see through me better than friends and acquaintances. Plus, for all I knew, any of them might have been told about what happened in that basement when I was six.

The wedding was big, lavish, and beautiful. White lace and dim lighting bathed the coliseum-like stone walls of the

50

elaborate Sea Island Cloister Hotel. The marriage ceremony had family and friends in tears, and sentimentality spread through the crowd like a whispering breeze.

I had never tasted a beer before. But I liked how pot made me feel, so I was sure a beer would make me feel good, too. So far, everything I wasn't supposed to do had helped me feel better about myself: pot, masturbation, and acting out. Why not try alcohol?

I followed two of my cousins to a wall of hedges that were whole without gaps or lapses of color. They crouched down a little bit and vanished into the bushes, as if the wall of leaves had opened up and swallowed them.

"In here," one of them whispered.

I ducked my head and felt around like a blind man into a hollow spot in the seemingly impenetrable wall of green. The air on the island was thick and warm, but inside a dense hedge, everything felt even hotter and more humid. When I hit the open space on the other side, I was able to breathe again.

One of the older cousins said, "Ewww, this is the bad stuff!"

"But it gets the job done better than any other beer. It's like 10% alcohol," the other cousin said.

I had no idea what they were talking about, so I just kept playing it cool.

"It's only good to shotgun," said the oldest cousin. "Have you guys ever done a shotgun?" he asked.

When I didn't know something, I stayed quiet.

"Steven goes first," he said. "Baby Mark probably doesn't know how to do it."

He was right.

"Watch Steven, Baby Mark. You're next!"

He shoved a key into the bottom side of the beer sending out a spew of white froth like a geyser and blasting a sound of release like a punctured tire.

Quickly grabbing the beer, Steven put the sheared tin hole against his lips, and in one smooth motion, while tilting his head back and using his thumb to flip open the part of the can you're supposed to drink from, he commenced to drink. Out of the sides of his mouth, beer flooded down his cheeks, pouring from his chin like a wild river before flowing down the front of his shirt. I could hear him gulping, and his eyes grew large, as if full. He pulled back with a jolt as though the beer had turned sour, and he began coughing while froth sprayed from his mouth.

Then, it was my turn. My face turned hot, and my hands grew shaky. I didn't know if I could do what I had just witnessed. One of my cousins pointed the can toward the swampy overlook and punched the side of it. Spewing toward the tranquil moonlight, the froth sparkled as it flew through the night air. The droplets fell like heavy snowflakes, and my heart sank with them as they hit the ground.

Reaching out my hands while putting my head down, the same way I had watched my cousin do it, I prepared myself. I momentarily halted as I smelled the pungent odor and felt the tinge of alcoholic bubbles penetrate and sting my virgin lips. Closing my eyes, I placed my finger behind the tab, and as I stood up straight, tilting my head back and flipping the can open, I unleashed the rapid flow of liquid. Like a blast from a super-soaker or water hose releasing a kink, the stinging bubbles shot forth, bypassing my mouth altogether, and filled my throat like a water balloon. Under pressure, my esophagus was forced open, and beer traveled freely into my belly. Before

I could think what was happening, the can was empty, and my shirt, like my cousin's, was soaked.

I didn't feel anything, but tears had filled my eyes and obstructed my vision. Immediately after, I was told to take another can to the dome and then one more. My stomach built up pressure and began to swell. I threw up with the violence of a blow hole burst open by the force of ocean spray. For a few moments, I regretted my decision.

"You'll feel better now that you spewed!" my cousin cracked in a slightly drunken southern drawl.

Steven was in his own misery, yacking like a sailor on leave.

After my stomach calmed down and quit contracting violently, I raised my head. I looked out toward the moonlight, and I felt my face melt into the salty, serene landscape that stretched without limit. My mouth watered, and my eyes felt loose, as my mind slid off with my balance. I caught my body against a mossy oak tree with big, rough, 800-year-old bark that made perfect hand holds, but I couldn't catch my mind. As the warm alcohol filled my veins, I slipped deeper into oblivion and faded just like the withdrawn colors of the marsh landscape at night. Then, I threw up again.

When I came to, I wanted to be held, but at the same time, I wanted to be left alone. I wanted to curl up at my mother's side and promise her I would never drink again. I wanted to feel her caress my sticky hair.

But I also never wanted to see her again. I wanted to be a grown-up, and I wanted to stay drunk. Sick and unhappy, yet happy and drunk, my feet seemed as confused and conflicted as my soul. I crawled through the bushes and emerged onto the asphalt that was damp from the hazy, humid night.

As we made it back to the wedding reception, I gained my footing, but I'd lost touch with all reality. I forgot where and who I was, and I didn't recognize my own family. Time slipped away, and I knew deep down that although I had no clue about my surroundings or myself, I was exactly where and who I wanted to be forever. Faded and alone.

Eventually, I came to understand that a calm reassurance penetrates the heart of the lonely in oblivion. Predictable misfortune and ephemeral, transient joy are commonplace in the lonely-hearted. But understanding the warm blanket of solitude and the dark mask of isolation doesn't sit well with everyone. Most people want predictable joy and rare misfortune. These people just don't understand that when you expect misfortune, you always win.

Loneliness sat well with me, and as long as I was faded, I was alone but safe.

TWELVE

DROPPED OUT

After that first experience with beer, it became my mission to be loaded anywhere and everywhere I went. I learned about whipped cream nitrous shots and would take them from the fridge anytime they graced the shelves (sorry, Mom). I would sit at the computer, looking at porn and huffing all the cans of compressed air dusters that we bought from office supply stores (sorry, Dad).

While I listened to the hum of my brain, decaying like jelly, I contemplated my next high. Friendships became unimportant unless drugs or alcohol were available. Drugs, alcohol, and girls became my sole things to focus on. They were the only things that helped me feel the way I was "supposed" to.

If drugs weren't available, I would achieve a high through something called asphyxiation. I would have my friends choke my neck, cutting off circulation to my brain just enough for me to fall on the ground and wake back up with a tingle coursing through my nerves. The friends who were looking for a real friend, something I couldn't be because I couldn't be myself, became distant. I had a new identity, or lack thereof, that I was chasing. The problem, of course, was that this identity was a lie. I didn't enjoy the high like some people; I simply enjoyed the escape.

I lost sight of using sports as an outlet. Athletic accomplishment didn't help me run and hide from my fears as well as drugs.

As my new false identity with drugs was forming, I was also becoming more obsessive and controlling in my relationships with girls. I used them to confirm an identity, so I'd do anything and everything to keep a girlfriend. I'd have killed to keep a girlfriend. Likewise, I'd have killed to stay high. Both were tools to me and nothing more.

At fifteen, I basically kidnapped my girlfriend Katie after her parents caught us having sex in her bedroom. As a consequence, they weren't going to let us continue seeing each other. But I needed Katie, not because I loved her, but because of how straight she made me appear. So when her parents caught us, there was only one option—take her from her family and bring her with me into my world of lies.

I had been held back one grade in elementary school, so I was in my freshman year and was ready to drop of high school. My family had a residence in Atlanta, too, and we were staying there at the time. So my plan was to run away to the beach with Katie. We would sell pot, surf, and party. To execute the plan, I had to steal a car for transport to the beach, pick my girl up after our parents were asleep and before they woke up, and procure a half pound of pot from my high school drug dealer.

The task would be hard, but once executed, Katie and I would be able to live on the beach, selling weed and doing whatever we pleased as whoever we wanted to be. Drugs and partying.

Around 2:30 a.m., I sneaked downstairs to stealthily commandeer my father's prized Mercedes. Once I got the keys, I had to somehow bypass the home security system without awakening anyone.

My excitement grew as I stood beside the only window that wasn't attached to the central alarm system. I slid it open and stood on the window sill as I tossed my bag of clothes onto the lawn.

In front of the window was a long string of thorny holly bushes. If I were to fall into them, they'd awaken everyone faster than the alarm system. So I leapt toward the front yard, sailing over the hollies, and gracefully landed near my backpack in the dew-covered grass. Success! I wiped my paws while the thrill and freedom settled into my bones.

The garage door was closed, and opening it mechanically would be too risky. I stood on top of the car and created a lever using a broom and basketball to pry the door open manually from the inside. Starting the engine was also too risky, so I placed the car in neutral and pushed it out of the garage and into the driveway. Unfortunately, our driveway had a huge turn that went straight up a steep incline. Therefore, I would have to start the engine before being entirely clear of risking exposure. I sat in the car for a moment, and with an ounce of reluctance and a pound of excitement, I cranked the engine and flew up the driveway, out of the neighborhood, and onto the highway to rescue my princess Katie—my saving grace. Not only did I have to get past my parents, but I had to evade the cops since I was driving with only a learner's permit.

I cranked up my Sublime CD as I cruised the forty-five minutes to Katie's house. She, too, had to evade an increasingly tight parental security system since it was only the week before that her father had caught us buck naked in her bedroom losing our virginity together (or so she thought).

With the tightened restraints that her parents had given her as a consequence for sleeping with her boyfriend within their well-structured Christian home, it was a narrow possibility that she could join me.

Regardless, we set the plan to meet at 3:30 a.m. right down the street from her house. At 3:35, I saw my young love emerge through the dark shadows with a large pink duffle bag in her hand. A warm feeling flooded my stomach. I leapt out of the car, ran toward her, and tried to hug her. But she was too stiff and frightened to utter a word until we had long left her neighborhood.

It was a distance back to my school, and for the most part, we remained quiet, in shock, listening to music, and trying to catch our breath. Once we got to the school's neighborhood, we found a semi-secluded cul-de-sac where we could park the car. I tried to make moves to have sex, but Katie was too nervous.

We sat in the car for the next few hours, waiting for students to begin arriving so that I could find my drug dealer and procure the bag of weed that would be our future. As the sun arose over the Atlanta skyline, we made small talk and entangled our dreams with our bodies, colliding with sweet kisses and soft caresses in the backseat.

A lifetime of waking up pain-free to sex and weed on the beach was cresting over the horizon. All I had to do was get into the school building, find my dealer, and evade school security. I had become a pro at doing this over the course of my freshman year; I knew all the ins and outs.

I had joined the football team, and I began practice the summer before school started. By the end of summer, before my first day of high school, I had a dealer, knew the places to smoke weed, and had built a reputation on the team as the crazy, angry white boy. I had respect in the hallways of the high school from the upperclassmen because I would be starting on the varsity football team as a freshman. A few days after school started, I was already being invited to skip school with seniors and smoke weed until returning after lunch break. This became my routine.

I started failing my classes, of course, but football was going well. So my coach helped me get some extra assistance. This meant, however, that I had to put forth effort that I was unwilling to make. Despite being allowed to take some exams alone and turn in homework a couple of days late, I continued to fail.

At this point, I had been removed from eight different schools, so I had little belief that this stint would last long, no matter how well football was going. Therefore, I don't think any of the teachers or students were surprised when I didn't show up for class on that spring day I decided to leave town with my lover.

As my father's Mercedes and the girl of my dreams waited outside for me to return with our financial future in weed, I became more and more filled with confidence. I was dropping into the exact life role and identity that were congruent with my beliefs about myself. At the beach, I would be able to live high, faded, criss-crossed, and so lost that I wouldn't even need to know my own name.

But when I got back to the car, Katie had a different train of thought settling in her soul. She no longer believed running away to the beach was the wisest idea. Luckily, it wasn't hard for me to help her change her mind. After all, no one would want to go home and face the consequences of running away.

We drifted down the road on pavement that felt smooth and worry-free as it led us winding gently around the hilly suburban neighborhoods of Atlanta toward the interstate. Once there, we would be home-free, but someone had a different plan for us.

As we crested around one of the last bends of the winding forested roads near River Wood High School, where we had secured our weed, I looked in the rearview mirror and saw my mother's car. It was barreling down the road like General Lee from the *Dukes of Hazard.* I put the pedal to the metal, but it wasn't nearly enough steam to evade a vehicle powered by a mother's love. She cornered us, and we had no choice but to stop.

"What are we going to do?" Katie asked in a panic.

"It's okay. We'll just talk to her and see what she has to say," I replied calmly. I knew if we didn't like what we heard, my foot was just one neuron-firing away from propelling us toward our dream destination. I rolled down the window as Mom approached the side of the car.

"Where are you guys going?" she said in a casual tone.

"We're going to Sea Island to get away for a little bit," I replied. I was confused by her calm tone and choice of words.

"Sea Island?" she asked. "Why didn't you just ask? I would have gladly taken you two down there."

I looked at Katie, and she looked back at me with her big, beautiful, kitten-like eyes. I shrugged my shoulders while she nodded her head and smiled.

"Katie, why don't you ride with me, and Mark, you can follow us and take some time to think," my mom said.

Sea Island was five hours away, so this was going to be a long time to sit and think. At least I had the weed.

"No, Katie can ride with me," I said.

"No, if Katie doesn't ride with me, you two won't be going at all."

Katie opened the door and gladly agreed. *What the hell?!*

By the time we got to Sea Island, I had done a lot of thinking and had conjured up a new plan. Katie, on the other hand, had received a lot of convincing mom-talk. I could tell her mood had changed.

We went for a walk on the beach and exchanged minimal words. I felt that I had lost her. The next morning, her parents were at the door and took her, willingly, back to Atlanta. My life fell out of control.

Losing Katie felt like the end of the world because it also meant I lost the identity I wished for and felt I deserved—an identity that would allow me to stay disconnected from the truth I knew inside.

Alone and weeping over my lost life and love, I stayed high for a few weeks and tried to convince my parents to allow me to drop out of school. After a couple of weeks out of school, they decided it may be best if I went elsewhere.

THIRTEEN

WILDERNESS & AFFINITY

My mother sat me down on the large, soft, yellow couch with cushions too big for the spots they occupied, causing them to balloon out like the distended belly of an aging diabetic. Out of the corner of my eye, the gas fire flickered, and its warmth caressed one side of my face. But the crackling that makes a fire so comforting was missing. I knew this conversation was going to be a serious one.

"What does marijuana do for you, Mark?" my mother asked.

I was stumped. I had a feeling she might be interested in trying it with me.

"I don't know. I just like it," I said with the pensiveness of a teenager holding back my inner child and embellishing my burgeoning adulthood (as teenagers do).

"Well, you must like it a lot. Do you think I would like it?"

I and sat up erect while trying to maintain my composure. All of a sudden, I felt uncomfortable, annoyed, and embarrassed, yet excited and nervous. These were the same conflicting feelings I had when the stereotypical "birds and the bees" talk came from my dad's reluctant lips.

"Well, yes, Mom, I think anyone would like it. But I think you might *really* like it. You seem like a person who would enjoy it. It makes music sound better and food taste better, and..."

"Well, how would I get it?" she interrupted.

"I could get you some right now. All I need is $20!" I was thrilled. My mom and I were going to share a joint together. Some of my friends had parents who smoked pot, and their relationships always seemed tight. Maybe after this, we could have that "cool mom and son" relationship that I thought I wanted.

"$20 isn't all that much, but how often do you need more?" she inquired.

I felt a shift in her interest, and I tried to pull it back to salvage what had been.

"Well, really, I only need $10, and you can make that last for a couple of days if you don't smoke much," I retorted.

"But if it makes everything better, wouldn't you want to smoke a lot so that you stay feeling great?"

"Well, sure, but that's not always possible," I responded.

"Sure it is, Mark. I remember only two or three years ago, seeing you happy all the time. You were so active—mountain biking, playing sports, meeting up with friends, playing in the woods," she said, as if trying to summon a lost child. "I know that you can find that same type of joy again—the type of joy where you don't need to spend $10 a day and you don't need to smoke."

My hope dissolved. The conversation had turned into the anti-drug talk I'd initially suspected. How did she twist this around on me? She knew I would leave immediately if she didn't start it off with something that grabbed my attention. My mother was both cunning and wise.

"That's why your dad and I thought you might like to take a couple months off from school and go to an adventure camp in the woods—a place where you can revisit the things you love and reignite your passion for nature and activity."

No school? No family? No relationships to keep up with?

"I know it's been hard for you to find joy after Katie left, and we just think this might be a great, fun thing for you to do."

She had me. It did sound great. So I agreed. "Okay, when do we leave?"

"Tomorrow. We already got your plane ticket, and your cousin Charlie is going with you."

"Tomorrow!? What if I had said no?"

"Well, we had a backup plan for that, so I'm just glad you agreed. It will be great! Charlie will be here at 4:30 in the morning. I'm so excited for you. You're going to have so much fun!"

The next thing I knew, after pondering all the tears and frustration of youth through the night, my cousin Charlie was sitting next to me on an airplane toward a new chapter of life. I would not be going back to high school. Instead, I was on a plane to a wilderness camp in Utah.

It was a treatment program that used the wilderness experience to challenge kids and, in a sense, force them into submission. It wasn't as my mother had described. It was a place of punishment.

Most kids got there and worked the treatment manuals to a T so that they could be released to go back home or to a therapeutic boarding school if they weren't completely fixed. The kids promised to change their ways, start behaving in school, and listen to their parents. Most of these promises fell on deaf ears, however, as the majority of them were shipped off to a boarding school. When I saw this happening to the others, I didn't make empty promises. The truth is that I just didn't have the aversion to solitude and wilderness life like most of them. I liked the desert and the seclusion from society. My attraction to the area most likely stemmed from the inspiration of my role model, Jim Morrison, who found solace and magic in the same neighboring desert. I idolized him.

So even though it was a place of punishment, I did end up seeing it to some degree as my mother had described—a fun and enlightening place where I could explore myself without the pressure of school and social involvements.

I picked mushrooms out of cow paddies and collected enough ephedra root from the plant, knowing if I made it into a tea, it could give me a jolt like ephedrine and turn life into light speed. I boiled the roots in my morning oatmeal and my evening rice and lintels, thus keeping myself in a nice, steady (albeit weak) psychedelic daze for the eight weeks they kept me there.

The program was only supposed to last for four weeks, but since I had been tripping around the desert with a general sense of contentment instead of the typical yearning drive to be released, they kept me for another four weeks. Then, they finally kicked me out.

Next, I was shipped off to a boarding school, where I didn't last more than a few weeks before I was kicked out for conspiring to burn the place down. My anger was becoming hot and powerful as fire.

From there, I was taken to a ranch owned by an older Christian couple. Sitting in the car on the way to this ranch, the drivers began talking about the program I was about to fall into.

"This place is going to be a little different from that horrible place where you were," the driver said with a sense of pride, like he was saving me. A man in the passenger seat with a flat-billed hat, huge dark tattoos, and a tight shirt concealing beautiful muscles concurred by nodding his head.

Even though I got into trouble there, I'd thought the last boarding school was pretty nice. I described it to the men in the car. They had great food, a climbing wall in the gym, and beautiful facilities. The school sat in the woods about twenty miles outside of Kalispell, Montana. When you drove up through the gates, it felt like you were approaching some oligarch's woodland mansion. The structures were a deep mahogany red, made of massive logs. The ceilings were high, the corridors were long, and the windows were huge. All of the furniture in the facility matched the outside. Thick, strong, and beautifully hand-carved log chairs and couches lined the hallways, and the dining room tables were so large that they were fit for Vikings. It felt more like a luxury forest retreat than a teen rehab.

"Well," the man with the tattoos said as he turned, exposing his endearing, strong masculine face to me, "it ain't as fancy as that posh place, but what you're gonna find at Affinity is a new type of rehab. The kids here treat the owners more like family. They even call them 'Mom and Dad.'"

Oh, God, I thought. This was going to suck. To be able to call someone Mom and Dad would require a lot of trust (or brainwashing). I was already nearing the point of calling my biological parents by their legal names. I had no trust, so I wasn't going to call anyone "Mom and Dad."

What type of incestuous place is this? I thought. But instead of saying it out loud, I asked, "So it's called Affinity?"

"Yeah, that's the name of the group home we're headed to. We both work there. It's a group home, unlike those big rehabs. The group home setting is more based in trust and God's love."

Most kids learn how to trust someone in their life before they reach their teenage years. But not me, and the secrets and pain kept adding up. If you never tell the truth and never open up, you can't build trust. Despite my loving parents and siblings, I ostracized myself. Therefore, I was as lonely as an abandoned child sweeping chimneys and stealing wallets and apples in Dickensian England.

I was not going to be able to fake trust, but with my experience in Christianity, this God thing would be easy for me to falsify while also resisting it.

The drivers who brought me to Affinity were right. When I arrived, I was shocked. In the morning, the kids came running to the kitchen and hugged the owners. I felt like I was intruding on someone's family.

For nearly a decade, this older couple took teens into their home to show how love, intimacy, and truth can bring healing to the most damaged of souls. They had kids there who had been through much worse than me. I could tell from how the other kids acted that the work at this place had a huge impact on them. When I first stepped onto the property, it horrified me.

My first week in the program, they were taking a "family trip" to a Christian music festival for more than a week, but as a new arrival, I wouldn't be invited to join them. I had to build more trust before going on these trips. The place was fairly short-staffed, and one of the other kids had to stay back, too. In his case, it was as a consequence for his poor behaviors.

The staff planned to take him deep into the woods and make him hike the whole time, and since there was no one available to keep an eye on me, I had to go along.

"Don't worry," said the burly older staff member in baggy camo pants and a tight black shirt. "You don't have to hike. You can sit in the car with me, and we'll get to know one another."

"How does that work if John is hiking?" I asked.

"Oh, we won't be far. We'll be in the car close behind him."

Oh, my God. This is sick, I thought. But I had no choice.

I sat in a car in the summer heat and watched this poor boy walk down a secluded forest road. He cried and huffed until he was too tired to continue. When he sat down and gave up, the burly man in the driver's seat yelled at him through cigarette smoke to get back up.

I felt heartbroken for John, so when we were returned to the campsite for the night, I decided to talk him into running away with me. It didn't take much convincing.

We left shortly after the burly man fell asleep. We just started walking with no food, very little water, no map, and no clue.

We walked through the night, loudly chanting "Hey, bear!" to hopefully spook any grizzlies into keeping away from us. We were still on the road when the sun began to come up, which meant burly man would notice our disappearance and come looking. So we started walking faster and with greater caution. Soon, we heard a train rumbling somewhere nearby through the forest.

"Perfect!" I said.

"Let's go hop the train!" John replied.

We smiled at each other and tore off through the woods toward the sound. We found the tracks and watched the train barreling down the steel beams fast as a car on a highway.

"I didn't think they went that fast," I said, dismayed.

"Me either," John said, as we both sat down to collect our thoughts.

Our feet were so tired, and our tummies were empty. We were now out of water and would soon be getting thirsty. But we had no choice but to continue.

"If we follow the train track, we'll eventually reach a town," I said.

We walked on that track for a day. As the heat built, our desperation grew. We both decided to drink our own pee.

Just when we were both ready to give up, we heard a car and took off toward it.

John suddenly halted. "What if that's Affinity staff looking for us?"

"Well, it's better than dying out here." I said.

When we got to the road, we saw that the man inside the truck wasn't from Affinity.

It was weird that he was sitting in his car with the engine on in the middle of nowhere Montana, but it didn't matter.

He turned toward us, shocked.

"What are you kids doing out here?"

"We're trying to get away from this guy who's making us stay out here," I said as we walked toward him.

"What do you mean? Like troubled youth?"

"Yes, sir," I replied.

"Well, I get that. I'm sort of on the run, too, but from the mafia in Chicago."

We were already within a few feet of his truck, so we accepted when he followed up his disconcerting comment with, "Would you kids like a ride?"

I can't express how good it felt to sit in his truck. My legs felt like daggers of fire after walking for nearly twenty-four hours straight. We were exhausted.

"Are you boys hungry?" he asked.

"Famished."

"Well, let's get to town, and I'll buy you some goods before you go on your way."

As he drove, he told us stories about the Chicago mafia, while skillfully avoiding the reason he was running from them. When we got to the store nearly an hour later, I was excited that this journey was almost done.

He bought us fishing rods, food, and supplies to make fires and camp. We were both beyond grateful when he handed us twenty dollars and said good luck.

"Man, that was interesting," John laughed as the man drove away.

"Fuck!" was all I could think of to say.

I reached into my pocket and pulled out cough medicine that I had stolen from the grocery store and asked John if he wanted some. He declined, so I took his portion, too. We ate our food and began walking down the street.

It was only about twenty more minutes before a police car pulled up. By that time, I was so disoriented from the cough medicine that I could barely stand up. The cop knew who we were, and we didn't have the energy to fight. So he cuffed us and hauled us to the Eureka County jail, where we waited until the Affinity staff came to collect us. To put it mildly, they weren't happy, so they drove us back to the forest, where we were thrown out of the truck near timber that had been cut by the forest service. I was still tripping and groggy from the cough medicine, but I could see that the timber was stacked higher than my shoulder.

Burly man shouted, "You're going to take each log, one of you in the front and the other in the back. You're going to march it for one mile, set it down, and come get the next log. You will do this until all the logs are at the new stack. Then, you'll repeat this and bring them back. We're going to do this for ten days while Steven watches from the car. I have to leave now because I'm so mad at you two that I'm scared I'll do something I'll regret!"

"Fuck," I said in disbelief.

"Fuck is right," Steven said. "I'm going to make sure you boys don't fuck around!"

Steven had just graduated from the program as a student and had been hired as a staff member. He was wildly excited to exert his power.

After ten days of shuttling the logs back and forth with Steven yelling at us, we were told we had succeeded at the first part of "Affinity-style wilderness," which was actually "Steven's-style wilderness." For the next part, we would both have to do what he called "solos."

"What are solos?" I asked, afraid to hear the answer.

"Solos are just as they sound, dumbass. I'm going to take you at least five miles from any road, and we'll set up a tent. I'll mark out a five-foot perimeter around the tent, and if you leave that perimeter, you'll have to start at day one with the logs. We have cameras in the trees, so we'll know if you leave your tent. You'll be alone in the woods for ten days."

My stomach dropped, and pools of sweat immediately filled my palms. *Was he serious?* I asked myself as I scanned his face. His expression showed no sign that he was joking.

"What about bears?" I asked.

"Haven't you read about Daniel in the lion's den?" he replied in a smartass tone. "Here's a Bible. You can read about it."

As he turned to walk away, he dropped the Bible on the ground along with a bag of rice and beans, a small stove, and a five-gallon jug of water.

"What if I have to shit?"

"Do it by your tent," he laughed and took off running down the trail.

The next ten days were nothing short of the loneliest, most horrifying days I've ever experienced. I dared not leave the five-foot perimeter, and fear became my only strength. But I survived, and at the end of those ten days, I was filled with hate and rage for Affinity. I'd had ten days of living in my head, though, so I was also filled with hate and rage for myself.

I had already been kicked out of the strict therapeutic boarding school, thrown out of a wilderness camp for troubled teens, and expelled from my home in Georgia after kidnapping my girlfriend and attempting to flee to the beach. I so badly needed people to finally just give up on me so that I could be as I saw myself.

So when I was back at Affinity, I did everything to make the staff give up on me. I cursed their God to their face. I sneaked around with forbidden girls every chance I got. I stole pain medicine from them, and when that was gone, I stole the cough medicine. And when that was gone, I stole some prescription medicine meant for one of the other youths. It ended up making me sick as a dog, blowing my cover. But they wouldn't give up on me and kick me out.

Then, an angel came into my life at Affinity. His name was Ryan.

I had been there a little over a year when he arrived. He came in shy. He was cute, and he seemed innocent. Tradition held that upon admittance, the newcomer would share a little bit of their story.

Ryan was open. He was a book worth reading, and it was written in large print. He didn't try to act cool. His story wasn't long like most of the kids at the rehab, though. Rather, he wrapped everything up in a couple of sentences.

"Well, my parents sent me here because I came out as gay." The boys looked around and smirked, and I twisted uncomfortably in my chair. "They are both very strong Christians. My dad is like the strongest firefighter man, who has a masculine aura that makes Thor seem pusillanimous." Ryan had a vocabulary that was robust but not yet mature. His attempts to create beautiful sentences captivated me, however, and I was instantly attracted.

"They sent me here because they couldn't handle raising a boy who was gay. The people in their church would disown them, and I would ruin everything."

I couldn't believe my ears. The confidence of this boy was exhilarating. I knew people who had come out of the closet, but no one who came out of the closet to parents like these. How did he do it? Could I do it, too?

It would take a few days for it all to settle in, but I would eventually let everyone in the group home know about me, too. I could no longer hide who I truly was inside, and they weren't going to let me go on to become the person I believed I was. So I divulged all the dirties to them.

When they knew my real identity—the boy who learned about sex at an early age from a family member close to him and later had gender identity issues and sexual tendencies toward men that were aberrant from the southern social norm—they didn't retreat. They grew closer and fonder. They wrapped their arms tighter around me and worked harder to help me, in their own way. But they saw our homosexuality as demon possession. One night I was surrounded by four Pentecostal priests who pinned me to the bed and shouted in tongues. They would only let me free if I asked Jesus to come into my life. It took a few hours until I finally let go and prayed with them.

It was things like this that caused Ryan and I to believe our sexuality was demonic, too. Nevertheless, because I spilled my beans when Ryan showed me it was possible, we instantly became more than friends. We were star-crossed lovers, but we dared not pursue it physically, given the house rules and the threat of going back to the wilderness or some other crude punishment. Instead, we acted as brothers for the remainder of our time at Affinity.

At this place, lies could prevent a person from graduating. So throughout the course of the program, we both made an honest effort to allow God to strip the demonic gayness from us and heal our relationship through prayer. But man, did we feed off each other!

He taught me vocabulary, math, and how to row on the ergometer like a champion. I taught him poetry, music, and the wonders of the outdoors—God's greatness in creation. I loved every moment with him.

Meanwhile, I did everything I had to do to get away from the people who now knew everything about me. The level at which they knew me scared me more than all the fears I had ever experienced. So I began lying again because that's what I did when I was in fear—I lied and put on a mask.

I began acting like a bona fide Christian youth warrior on fire and a boy in recovery from gayness. I mentored the new students. I never cussed, never complained, woke up early, and got the house ready for all the other kids. I ran and worked out before anyone got up, and I even fed the cows most mornings before sunrise. I made a point to be the star of the group home, and within a few months, I was headed home. I had succeeded. For the first time, I was leaving a place with an honorable mention; I hadn't been kicked out.

FOURTEEN

TRIPPING

Between the boarding school and Affinity, I had spent three years in youth rehab, consisting of behavioral modification with a Christian focus. I was eighteen years old by the time I left.

I knew how to act based on what was demanded from others, but I didn't know myself any better. I don't blame the programs or the people who owned them for the maltreatment of some of their staff. Plus, the psychological industry didn't really know how to handle troubled youth at this time. They tried the best they could, and I saw that after time. By the end, in fact, I had grown to love the family at Affinity and began to view them as my own kin. But these programs didn't help me connect with my new sober-minded identity as much as they helped me connect with their ideals. So when I came out of troubled youth living, I was still searching for who I was and who I could be.

Throughout my youth, I had identified what I liked based on what other people liked. I chose my hobbies because they were the same hobbies of people whose time I cherished. My ambitions were the same as the ambitions of people I idolized.

After being in the group home, my own true preferences were confused, and my ambitions had become the same as my parents and the authorities at Affinity. Everything I'd learned about myself in these programs was based on how to please the people who held the keys to my graduation and release from the program. By reading how others failed in the Christian life, I learned how I could succeed.

Ultimately, I became a master emulator of moral resonance and an actor in a play with a centuries-old script. If I showed up in the right places with the right face, things would work out for me.

I might have even become a straight preacher in Oklahoma rather than a gay triathlete in Colorado, had there not been one particular problem: my foundation was built on the cornerstone of others' beliefs and a lie in my own heart. I was taking another person's prescription for an ailment I knew I didn't have.

At that point, I knew I was gay, and all I wanted to do was to come out. The drive to express my true sexuality became harder to repress. But at the same time, I was still hopeful that somehow, God might take it away.

Meanwhile, I became a youth intern at a church in Brunswick, Georgia and moved back in with my family on Sea Island. On the outside, everything looked cool.

The experience at the church was great, but since this persona of a pastor teacher was an embellishment of what other people wanted from me and not what I wanted for myself, it quickly lost flavor. Having nowhere else to run for some semblance of an identity, I once again discovered my good friend, Mary Jane: the devil's weed.

When I was caught selling it to the youth pastor's son, my job ended abruptly. So then, I became a lifeguard, which I loved. I could smoke all the weed I wanted, meet all the girls I wanted, and check out all the boys I wanted—while keeping shades over my eyes.

As this lifestyle became more ingrained, however, I began to feel defeated. I knew I didn't actually want most of what I was doing. I didn't want to keep acting straight. I didn't want the girls. I didn't want the drugs. I simply used them to forget and to hide. But inevitably, the high disappears, and there you are left with yourself.

I began to feel devalued and worthless. While searching for an outlet, I learned about the ease and availability of mobile and virtual sex. So I set up a personal profile on a few adult websites and began sending pictures, making videos, and performing phone sex with strangers.

It was an exhausting way to live.

Then, one night, the drugs acted against me, and I couldn't hold back what was on the inside.

It was a hot and humid day in autumn. Early in the morning, my friends and I packed a garbage bag and planned a trip inland to some cow pastures. Our goal was to collect as many mushrooms as possible and have ourselves a wonderful psychedelic night. We were loading up in the car when my phone rang.

"Mark?" said the voice on the other end. "You know you're supposed to be the lifeguard today, right?"

"Fuck! Oops—I mean, sorry! I'll be there in ten minutes."

I couldn't lose my job. If I did, I would have to work as a

survey assistant in my dad's engineering company. While that wouldn't have been so bad, it wouldn't carry as many pleasures as being a lifeguard.

"I'll meet you guys after work," I told my friends. "Ya'll gonna be here?"

"Yeah, here or Cortez's house."

Cortez was a friend who was one of our go-to's for a high. If you even so much as touched him, there was a chance you would start tripping. He was also able to always save face, no matter how deep the situation might have become. I rode in his car with him once on a crystal-clear night, when all of a sudden, he started rubbing his eyes with vigor.

"Cortez, you all right, dude?" I shouted through the piercing guitar solos of Phish that were bouncing off the tin walls and glass windows of his Honda.

In a cool response that I'll never forget, he said, "Yeah, man, I just feel like the car is sinking into the pavement, and I can't see anything. What's up with this damn green fog?"

"What the fuck, Cortez? What are you on?"

"Uh, just a little bit of LSD, mescaline, and a quarter ounce of mushrooms," he said like it was nothing. "But I'm fine, man. My eyes are just a little dry."

I stared at him as he held onto the steering wheel and gracefully kept us straight as an arrow, cruising down the road like low riders. *Man,* I thought. *I wanna be like this guy.*

The last time I had eaten a quarter of mushrooms, I sat on the side of the street wearing only underwear and holding my shoes full of sand. I had run out of a party because I thought a girl was trying to sleep with me, and all I wanted was a guy I had a crush on. I had spent the majority of my mushroom trip curled up in a ball on the beach and looking for "my identity" by digging holes in the sand. Surely it was down there somewhere.

I didn't find it while digging on the beach, but the night after I had to leave my friends to return to my lifeguard job, I kind of did find it—at least for a brief moment.

When I found my friends again that night, they had mushrooms scattered across the entirety of an 8x10-foot tarp, with less than an inch between each one. My jaw dropped to the floor.

"Jesus Christ!" I said. "How the hell did you guys get this many mushrooms?"

"Dude, it was a freaking perfect day!" my good friend Colin shouted as he lit a cigarette and dangled it from his lips. Colin was the coolest guy I knew. He was drop dead gorgeous, he used to live in New Orleans, he had connections for all sorts of drugs, and he didn't have to work. His experiences enthralled me.

"Hurry and eat some. We all just ate a bunch!" my friend Sam chimed in while lighting his own cigarette. "We're going to have one hell of a trip tonight!"

The problem was that I had a difficult time eating mushrooms. I didn't like the texture, and I hated the taste. I either needed tea or peanut butter to get them down. Luckily, they had both.

The tea had been simmering for an hour or two. As the liquid streamed into my cup, it had an opaque purplish hue that looked like the royal silk robe of an old English king. After I filled my cup, I set it aside to cool while I ate my first couple of raw, soggy, sloppy, southern, brown cow dung mushrooms with spoons full of peanut butter. I had eaten quite a few when Colin said, "All right, guys, now I've got the main course."

Hmm … I thought mushrooms were to be the main course. *What does this sexy man have up his sleeve for me tonight?*

He looked down, his cigarette carefully placed in the corner of his pursed lips, inhaling as he reached into his pocket. "I was just down in New Orleans, and I scored some high-quality mescaline-laced ecstasy. My brother David and I tried them. They are *fire!*"

Fire was a word that meant the drug did what it was supposed to do in an excellent way. It was the word you wanted to hear before taking a drug.

He handed me a small round pill, which I plopped into my mouth. Sam took one, too, and immediately took off in his little blue car, racing home to do some things before the trip set in.

The sun was going down. The warmth of the day was lifting, and the humidity stuck around like a warm, wet, satin cloak draped on my skin.

Down south, when the sun goes down, relief always comes with it as if something caged inside is set free. You don't feel as vulnerable. But if you have spent the whole day outside baking in the sun as I did as a lifeguard, the animal that's caged inside is just plain sleepy.

Colin and I opened the door that led from the mushroom den garage into his mother's home. His brother was on the couch in boxers, watching a movie. Colin jumped over and punched him in the arm, a brotherly expression that really meant, "I'd like to sit down next to you." While David shuffled over and punched Colin back, I found my way into a chair in the corner of the room that had a good view of the TV.

They're cute boys, I thought.

The large, white cushioned chair held me like an oversized bean bag with loving arms, so before I knew it, I was asleep as the drugs entered my system.

Suddenly, I awoke, but I couldn't move. I'd forgotten where I was, and I had no idea how long I'd been asleep. It was pitch dark outside, so it must have been a while.

I looked over at Colin and his brother, forgetting that they were brothers. All I saw were two boys. I wanted to join them on the couch, but I couldn't move. I lay back into the chair and into the warm satisfaction that boiled through my veins with mescaline, psilocybin, and ecstasy. My eyes rolled back into my head, and I lost consciousness again.

"Mark!" I heard a familiar woman's voice cascade through my dream and into my head, with a distressing tone of desperation. "Mark, please!" It was louder that time, as if the voice was getting closer. "Mark, not now!"

The voice was then recognizable as my mother's. She was so close that I could feel her breath in my dream. "It's not your time! Please don't go!"

I tried to wake up, but I couldn't open my eyes. I was stuck. I must have overdosed, and my mother was trying to save me.

My heart raced, and I started to panic. Was I in a coma?

Bam, bam, bam! My chest pounded as if it were the biggest drum in the middle of a pow-wow.

"Please bring him back!" I heard Mom's voice wail, slightly farther away than before and muffled due to the interference of outsiders banging on my chest.

Bam! Crack! My ribs broke, and I convulsed.

"Is this going to work?" my mother cried. "Is CPR all you can do?!?"

"Ma'am, please step back. We're taking him to the hospital and will do our best."

I felt myself glide through the air, each second marked by a *bam!* over my chest, sending a shock of fear deep inside me.

Bam! This time, it was steel doors and then a poke in my arm. "Ouch!"

Bam! I felt something on my chest as I heard wheels screech, and cold metal touched my chest.

"Is his heart beating?" my mother asked. She must've gotten into the ambulance.

Thank God she's here. I'm so scared.

"*Sorry, Mom,*" I said to myself, through my shut lips. "*I'm sorry. I know I shouldn't have taken so many drugs at once. Will you forgive me? Can you save me? Help me, Mom. I'm so scared. I don't want to die.*"

Beeep. I heard the tone that I feared more than anything. It was the notorious end-of-life chime. But this chime had a rhythm. I still had a chance. *Beeeeep.* That one was longer.

"Please, Mom, I can't die. I love you and need to hug you. I need to see you!"

"Mark, stay with us!!" she yelled as the beep got longer. "Please don't go, Mark."

Beeeeeeeeeeeep. The last beep trailed off with the wails of my mother's cry.

Instantly, my spirit launched out of the chair as if it were fighting to keep out of hell itself, with my body barely attached to the jump from death. The two boys I had just thought about sexually were no longer boys. A creepy smile stretched out, red and big as a slice of watermelon, across one of their faces. His eyes glowed a red, undulating ember that was more hot than

83

warm. His skin was brown and worn like a man climbing out of the trenches of World War II, but his hair was perfect. His clothing was radiant.

"Welcome back, Mark. It's been a long time," he said with a devilish tone that made my skin pull back tightly against my bones.

"Where am I?" I asked, barely able to stand. Pacing, I waited for his answer.

He stared at me. The other one, still sitting down, didn't seem to be paying attention at all.

"Are you okay?" he asked. His voice was hollow and deep, yet somehow endearing. I stared back at him, frightened. *Who was this devil? Where was I?*

"Did you die?" he said, his laughter shaking the souls of my feet and prompting the other one to stand and chime in.

"I don't think he's okay with all this," he stated before walking out of the room.

All this? What is all this? What the hell was going on?

"Let me call Satan," I thought I heard him say.

"No!!!" I yelled as I jumped toward him. "I'll change."

"Don't touch me!" he hollered back, sending me into retreat like a scared cat.

Then, all of a sudden, it made sense.

I loved men, and I couldn't *not* love men. I was in purgatory, and this demon was enlisted to send me to the flames for my transgressions, after he got clearance from Satan.

I had to act quickly. If he picked up his phone, he would call Satan, and I would be in hell. God, I wish that the CPR had worked. But maybe there was a small chance that I could contact God and make amends.

As I ran from the room, the guy tried to grab me, and I dropped to the ground.

"No, please! I'm not ready!"

"What do you mean?"

"I'm not ready to be here."

"Too bad. You're here now. Try to calm down."

I moved farther away, thinking that if he touched me, he would cause me to vanish into dust.

I ran into the foyer of the house. It was a beautiful room—circular, with a large chandelier towering above an expansive marble floor that connected three rooms, each with doors the height of giants. I found the middle of the marble and dropped to my knees, yelling, "Jesus!!! Please forgive me!!!"

I heard screams from the other end of the house. The demons tasked with sending me to hell didn't like this.

"Jesus," I yelled again. But there was no answer, and the demons' footsteps thundered toward me.

Jesus didn't come. So I ran from the demons, found a window, and threw myself outside.

Luckily, the window was only about ten feet high, and I landed on soft, thick, southern fescue grass that had been moist from the marsh and humidity all day. I felt relieved when I lifted myself off the ground.

I could breathe, but I was still dead. One of the demons shouted out the window, "Don't come back, crazy mother fucker."

Of course, there was no demon. It was my friend warning me not to come back. I was threatening the enjoyment of his trip, too.

But believing it was a demon, it was fine with me that I

didn't return. So I continued walking around, exploring my new home in eternity.

After a few hours, the psychedelics began to wax and wane, like they do. One minute, the universe was colliding in colors, dreams, and visions, as my legs felt like noodles. The next minute, I glimpsed reality, caught my breath, and understood where I was. During those glimpses, I was able to make my way back to the house from which I'd run.

Upon arrival, I found my two friends standing outside, each smoking a cigarette. I asked if I could have one and joined them in silent reflection. Upon inhaling the cigarette, the trip came back with a vengeance, and I lost the power of withholding.

I mumbled while pacing back and forth to the rhythm of my cigarette inhalations.

"I have something I have to tell you guys," I finally said. I thought if I said something, I would be able to settle into my skin.

"Jesus, what is it Mark? It seems like you've had one hell of a trip," Sam said. "I haven't seen you this whole time."

"I know, man; I had a really bad trip."

Colin laughed, "No shit. You kept calling me a demon."

"I just have something weighing on me that I have to get out."

I kept pacing back and forth.

"Well, what is it?" Sam said. "Maybe you'll feel better after you say it."

"I'm gay," I blurted out.

There was silence for a brief moment in which all stood still. All was remembered, fears were felt, joys were missed, and tears were lifted. This must be the way it feels to be suddenly squished by a life-sized iron anvil. A moment where all comes back and all disappears, right before everything becomes new again.

I couldn't wait to discover what was on the other side. Right as the laughter came forth, I rescinded my statement. "Just kidding!"

But it was out, and both of them saw through me.

"It's okay, Mark. I knew you were gay, you sexy thing," Sam said in his own shitty way that rubbed me in all the right and wrong ways.

"Are you into Colin?" he cracked.

"No! I'm kidding. I'm not gay," I lied.

I had a crush on both of them.

FIFTEEN

RYAN

A couple of weeks after the bad trip and my confession, I received a phone call while I was in my car. My caller ID read "Seattle, Washington." I only knew two people from there. One of the guys was a part of my troubled crew at the first boarding school. There was no way he had my number. The only other person it might be was Ryan, but that was farfetched, as he wasn't graduating from Affinity for at least a couple of months. But he had a way with words, so maybe he talked his way out of the place.

"Hello, this is Mark."

"Mark?" a still boyish voice echoed back.

"Yeah, is this ..."

"It's Ryan!" he completed my sentence, which wasn't unusual. I was thrilled, but I didn't know how to respond.

"I'm out of Affinity!"

"Well, I figured that, dude. How the hell did you get out so soon?"

"Dude, I just started working really hard right when you left the program, and they let me graduate with the next class."

What took me two years took him less than a year. But I don't know why I was so surprised. He was a charmer, and everyone loved him. The only thing "wrong" with him was that he was attracted to men. I loved him so and wished I had his light-footed step and innocent approach to life to take some of the lead out of my shoes.

He was one of the few people on this earth who, without a shadow of a doubt, understood me. We often talked while staring deeply into each other's eyes. We talked about philosophers like Socrates (Ryan was obsessed with Socrates), and we talked about meaning, purpose, and happiness. Sometimes, we even delved into the dark works of Voltaire and Dante with our innocently irrational minds.

"I'm in an eighteen-wheeler cruising through Alabama right now. I'm headed to you. Where do I need to go next?" he asked me.

"What!?" I jerked my car to the side of the road to catch my breath.

This wasn't good. I wasn't in a great spot. Ryan was fresh out of Affinity and had never done drugs. At that point, I was taking opioids daily and suffering withdrawal if I didn't have them. I had pill bottles full of Xanax, Lortab, Valium, and speed. I had bags of mushrooms, marijuana, and ecstasy hidden throughout my parents' house.

I was playing it cool, so they had started to trust me. But with Ryan coming to visit, I would have to hide it all from him. Yet, I knew I couldn't hide anything from Ryan, and he was sure to think less of me when he found out.

Screw it. He needs to know what he's getting into.

"If you get to Jacksonville or Savannah or Brunswick, I can pick you up," I said.

I heard him repeat the city names to the truck driver, and a muffled, raspy voice said, "Brunswick, yup."

"He said we'll be passing by the exit to Brunswick, and there's a truck stop strip club he stops at every time." Ryan laughed and continued, "Can you meet me there?"

I knew the place he was talking about because we often picked mushrooms at a farm right next to it.

"When are you guys gonna make it there?"

I heard some more muffled conversation, and Ryan responded, "Just a few more hours!" Then, he continued in a more monotone, serious voice. "Just don't tell your parents to call mine. My parents don't know where I am. We can tell them after a couple of days. I just want to see you. I need you right now."

I was both jacked and extremely nervous. I was so excited to see my soulmate, my brother, my best friend in the whole world. But he needed me? What did I have that could possibly help him?

I took some Xanax to calm my nerves and drove down the coastal streets of Sea Island, watching the tunnel of deep green, mossy oaks overhead. When I pulled up to my house, it hit me. What was I going to tell my parents?

But the Xanax eased my mind enough to figure it out. I was going to give Ryan drugs, and I was going to give him sex. I was going to show him what had been working for me, and I was going to feed lies to Mom and Dad.

"Ryan is coming into town tonight," I said coolly,

"Isn't he from Washington?" my mother said.

"Yeah, but his parents bought him a plane ticket so that he could take a vacation before heading to college." The lie was perfect. Every good parent does something like that, right?

"When does he get in?" my dad asked.

"I'll pick him up at 7:30 right after dinner. We probably won't be back until you guys are asleep. I'm going to take him to the beach first, so you can say "hey" to him in the morning. He'll sleep in the back of the house with me."

The back of the house had its own entrance. No one would hear when we got back, and no one would know what was going on back there. It was the perfect place for me at the time. I slept very little and needed a bed where I could bring my sexual partners. The back of the house was like a one-man Amsterdam brothel. I had a new sexual partner nearly every night and tons of drugs.

After dinner, I popped some ecstasy and a Valium before hopping into my Jeep Cherokee and cruising toward the truck stop meeting spot, which was about thirty minutes away. The combination of the two drugs kept me calm, but I felt super sensual, attentive, and talkative. Ryan was already there when I arrived, standing alone in the parking lot. I flickered my lights, and he ran toward my car with no bags in his hands.

I was still a little on edge, so I didn't jump out for a hug. Plus, this truck stop was the most sketchy spot on I-95, the major drug trafficking artery between Jacksonville, Florida and Georgia. I rolled my window down and shouted, "How the hell did you get here?!?"

He, too, was so excited that he lost himself and began telling me the story rather than jumping in the car. "I left Seattle. I couldn't stay at my parents'…"

"Get in the car, goober. Let's get out of this sketchy trucker strip club."

He made his way hastily around the front of the car, making eye contact with me and smiling as he kept a hand on the hood like a person gawking in a new car lot. He opened the door and said, "You know, truck stops and truckers aren't all that sketchy. I used to think so, too. But that's how I got here!"

"You hitchhiked the whole way?"

"Yes, I did!"

Part of me found him crazy for that, but the other part of me found the story to be irresistible and cute.

"You came all the way to see me?"

"I didn't know where else to go," he continued. "My parents wouldn't let me be gay, and I didn't want to ruin their lives."

"Oh, Affinity didn't fix your gay?"

"Nope! Not a bit."

"Me either." We glanced at each other, smiling and laughing. Then, we both leaned in for a kiss. He smelled like shit. "Let's get you home to a shower," I said, grabbing a baggy out of the center console. "And here's some ecstasy."

"What's it like?" he asked.

"Well, it makes all the colors brighter, makes sounds better, and it's supposed to make sex amazing. But I don't use it for sex because it makes me gayer than gay."

He laughed, and I laughed as he put his hand on my thigh, making me press it toward the gas pedal.

"So you're still in the closet?"

"Yes!" I said. "Well, at least I'm trying. I accidentally came out while I was high the other night. Look, you don't have to try the ecstasy. I've been taking it most nights all summer, so it doesn't affect me like it will you."

Ryan stared at me with a look of respect, care, innocence, and bliss. "Why don't we save your first time for tomorrow night?" I suggested.

"Okay."

We blabbered away and caught up on our news, revisiting some memories and expressing how we felt about one another.

"I love you, Mark. I have since the day we met,"

"Dude, I love you, too. I wish I was out of the closet like you are so that we could date."

"Well, we still kind of could, right?"

"I suppose, but you live out in Washington, and I'll be going to Tennessee for college."

"Yeah, I know. I'm going to have to go back home in a couple of days. Even though I hate my parents right now, I still love them to death, and I can't stand to hurt them. That's why I left, and it's also why I have to go back. Mark, I have no idea what to do. I can't stay, and I can't go."

"We'll try and sort it out over the next couple of days," I replied. "Maybe they'll be understanding after you've been gone like this."

"Yeah, maybe. Doubtful, though," he nodded, sounding hopeless. "It's been getting pretty rough at home."

He pulled his hand from my thigh. I slowed down and clumsily reached over to grab his hand. I finally caught hold of his pinky and ring finger, and I pulled them back toward my thigh.

"Let's do this, Ryan. I love you."

We drove the rest of the way in silence.

After his shower, we made love. This was his first time going all the way with another man.

"I feel guilty," he said after. He pulled up his pants. "We shouldn't do this again."

That was a feeling I knew all too well. So I gave him some Valium, and after a short period of time, our eyes got heavy. Then, we fell asleep together.

I awoke in the middle of the night, deep in thought. Guilt like this shouldn't come from something so beautiful and so natural. After all, if we abstained from drinking water, we would all die of thirst.

The next morning, we walked on the beach, and Ryan smoked his first joint. After that, we took some opioids and frolicked in the calm waves. We were free—laughing, happy, and high.

The three days that followed were a blur. We took about $400 worth of ecstasy and didn't sleep a wink. Our final night, we tripped on acid and made love under the stars on the beach.

Then, I had to take him to the airport. We got there two hours early, so we spent time together in the car. But before he left, I passed out from sheer exhaustion.

When I woke up about six hours later, he was gone. While I cruised home, I rolled down the window. Suddenly, a note hovered into the air above the dashboard, hit the windshield, and moved straight toward the open window. I caught it before it was sucked out.

The note was short and sweet: "You fell asleep and wouldn't wake up. I tried everything, even kissed you. I love you. I'll talk to you soon. –Ryan"

When I got home, my mother was waiting. Something was dreadfully wrong. "Why were you at the airport for six hours?" she asked.

"I wasn't," I said. "I dropped Ryan off and went to the beach."

My dad was standing near us. "No, you didn't. I followed you to make sure Ryan got there in time, since ya'll didn't come home last night. I watched you sit there without air conditioning for six hours."

"Are you using drugs again?" my mom asked, with a worried but not angry expression.

"Of course not!" I yelled and stormed out the back door, dashing across the small courtyard between the main house and the backside living quarters. I flung open the door, and when I saw the bed where Ryan and I had made love, I started crying.

I heard a knock on the door, and my mother walked in.

"So I heard you and Ryan had sex?"

"What are you talking about?!"

"Ryan told his parents, Mark, and they told us." She stared at me with a loving sort of scrutiny and kept talking. "They said when he got home, he was in really low spirits. Does this mean you're gay?"

"Mom, leave! Of course not!" If I wasn't already defensive toward my parents as a youth, I was overly so in that moment.

"Well, just know, God forgives you."

"Get out!" I screamed.

Finally hearing me, she crossed to the door, which creaked open. As she slinked her slender body through, she said one last crushing thing.

"Don't worry; I won't tell your father."

Those words echoed between my ears and landed in the empty spot that the ecstasy had left in my brain.

I understand why Ryan told his parents. He wasn't like me—the type to hide things in the closet. Plus, if he was in the same condition as I was after a week of partying, he didn't have the energy to hold anything back. Ecstasy binges have the side effect of severe depression. After a week or so of seeing colors so bright they touch your soul and hearing music so crisp it tickles your ear drums, normal life is disappointing and humdrum.

I was feeling good after my time with Ryan—even proud of it. So I had contemplated coming out to my parents. But when my mother walked out the door, saying, "Don't worry; I won't tell your father," everything changed. My heart sank. The entire world shifted from pride to shame, so I let the depression pull me deeper into darkness. After popping a few Valium, I fell asleep.

SIXTEEN

RYAN FLIES AWAY

A few weeks after Ryan left, I was checking into a small Christian college called Lee University in Cleveland, Tennessee, but I was starting to deeply regret that decision. I wanted nothing to do with the church. All I wanted were drugs and sex—to forget that I was gay and to never let my father find out. So I planned on doing very little school work.

Then, one night, I received a phone call: "Seattle, Washington" read the caller ID. I took the phone to my dorm room, kicked off my shoes, flung myself on my bed, and answered while plopping my head back on the pillow to look at the ceiling and dream as I listened to Ryan's voice.

He explained a new psychedelic trip he'd discovered, which was a combination of several different drugs. He said it was similar to Ayahuasca, a South American Shaman-type experience, only chemically induced through psychotropic pharmaceuticals.

"I'm going to send you a package with the instructions and all the ingredients in it. When you get it, call me, and we'll take it together. We'll find each other on another plane. It'll be amazing!"

"Is it safe?" I wondered out loud.

"Yeah, totally. But you have to follow the directions exactly because the order that you take the drugs is important."

"Okay. This sounds awesome! I can't wait to see you on the other side."

A week later, my package arrived. I ran back to my dorm room to open it. Inside were different pills with numbers on them, a little baggy filled with yellowish crystal shards, and a small note with the instructions.

I looked back down at the pills and the shards, and I thought about my day ahead. It wasn't a good day for tripping, so I decided to get back to Ryan after the weekend. The next day, I was heading to a music festival, and I didn't want to take away from that experience with a trip that could last a couple of days. So I placed the pills and the bag full of yellow crystals in my dresser.

The music festival was long and hard on the mind and body, causing me to sleep for a few days after we got back.

Then, a phone call came while I was relaxing, probably watching a movie. I don't remember who it was on the other end of the phone, but the news left me broken.

Ryan was in a coma. He had taken a psychedelic drug, along with a mix of prescription pills and was on life support. It was most likely the same concoction we were going to take together.

I should have called to let him know I wouldn't be able to take the drugs until the following weekend. I was beyond heartbroken, and it's still hard to forgive myself.

It was just a few weeks before they took him off life support. My love had died, and my secret went with him.

It would be years before I let the word "gay" come out of my mouth again.

SEVENTEEN

SWEET CAROLINE

After Ryan's death, I went into a coma of my own and spent about a year mostly highly on speed, ecstasy, and cocaine. My subconscious mind blocked my identity entirely, and I hid it so far inside me that I nearly forgot about my struggles with homosexuality. For the next few years, the only time I wrestled with any of those thoughts was when I got too high. Through a cocaine fog, I would become paranoid that people knew I was gay. I believed they could hear my thoughts.

Sometimes at parties, I'd have irresistible gay urges and go into the bathroom to touch myself in the way I imagined another man might touch me.

When most people are high on those drugs, they fraternize and become intensely jolly. Other guys liked to have sex on ecstasy and cocaine. But I became socially withdrawn and couldn't perform with women. At that point, my lies were beginning to hold me back from having fun with drugs. The party seemed to be over.

Then, along came Caroline. She's the woman who stole the thunder away from my lurking sexual proclivity toward men. She embodied sex, beauty, and life. Her very soul tore through mine and made an intimate home within me. I thought she was my rescuer. I thought I had been saved.

With long blond hair and legs that made runway models look drab, she would walk into a room, turning every eye her way. Her beauty was immense, but her presence was even more so. Her laughter was so genuine and pure that it could turn the lights on in a dark house. She made everything brighter.

I didn't have to hide when she was around, and for a while at least, I didn't feel like I had anything left to hide. I thought she'd cured me.

We went to music festivals, made love under the stars on LSD, and made visual music with our minds as our bodies collided and sent our spirits to a plane somewhere divine. We would hang out in bed for hours with our hands together and slowly pulling them apart until we experienced a web of connection like plasma strings in the universe. The strings would then tighten and pull our hands back together. We were struck and stuck in each other's stare.

The drugs had become fun again.

The love we made couldn't be replicated. It never will and never has. Reading love stories was disappointing because I knew no one, anywhere, at any time had ever shared a love like we shared.

We lived in a small house right outside of the Lee University Campus. After a semester, it was our goal to move to the University of Montana, a place that embodied our developing progressive/liberal mindset and, more importantly, our partying.

Once the semester was complete, we left, but my parents agreed to pay for my apartment only if Caroline didn't live with me. So we got separate places in our new town, and the physical separation caused us to drift apart. With the distance, my mind had time to be alone and remember who I was. I caught myself watching gay porn again. The confusion made me angry because I truly thought I was over it!

My inner conflict prevented me from seeing eye to eye with Caroline. It kept us from connecting the way we had before. Our arguments were like landslides crashing and destroying everything in their wake. We loved hard and fought even harder. In those fights, words were said that broke us, but it wasn't because of her. I was fighting her because of how angry I felt that she hadn't healed my gayness.

I was devastated after this breakup, and very quickly, I became hooked on sedatives. They helped me forget my struggles enough to attend class and not flunk out of school. They blocked my anxiety that people would find out I was gay.

Since I had my own apartment, I could have guys over for quickies. Then, when my friends came over, I could act straight as long as I was sedated. I got myself into a new cover-up relationship with a very loving girl, but I began sliding deeper and deeper into my addiction to sedatives. Then, I started mixing them with alcohol, and soon, opioids stole the thunder of my life.

This was around the end of my sophomore year of college.

EIGHTEEN

PROSTITUTION & HEROIN

Shortly after I graduated from Affinity, I found a website called Adult Friend Finder, and I set up an account. Using both Adult Friend Finder and Craigslist personals, I began interacting with anyone around the country willing to have virtual sex, and I sent them pictures of me.

Back then, I was able to turn intimacy into objectivity and still receive pleasure. Most of all, though, I experienced a thrill. I did webcam shows for people, performing in ways that turned them on. Occasionally, a man, woman, or couple would be in the vicinity, and I would meet them in person.

One woman I met gave me large amounts of pills each time I came over and fulfilled her fantasies. There were men who offered me money if I let them give me a blowjob. In return, I felt desired and worth more than I ever had.

I stayed very active on the websites until I met a girl who was willing to date, but it wouldn't be long until dating wasn't enough. Then, I would be back on the prostitution websites behind my girlfriend's back.

The prostitution carried on throughout my college life at varying degrees of intensity. It hit an all-time high when my drug dealing ran into a brick wall at the same time my heroin addiction reached a new summit.

Heroin addiction stripped my soul of any remaining morals and values. I did everything I could for the high the drug provided. I would sell everything I had, including my body. Then, I started stealing from homes around the university. I would wait until someone in the library left their book bag to go to the restroom and quickly snatch it in order to sell their books and anything else inside that someone would pay for. I was willing to drink sludge off the floors of a bar if it would help me get high. If it had been necessary, I would have killed someone.

But sex was easy. I tossed it around like a clown juggling hacky sacks.

Without the drugs, I felt as if I was knocking on heaven's door. Withdrawal sent blood-pounding heat through my veins that felt like it would scar my insides. My heart felt like a drum beating through armor while I nestled in a trench listening to a bomb every second throughout a long night of war, knowing I could blow up at any moment. I needed the sex, I needed the money, and I needed the drugs to survive.

I had a friend who worked at one of the porn stores in town, and she told me guys came in throughout the day to get their rocks off. At night, they flooded in. So I saw an opportunity and hopped on it like a starving tiger on prey.

I had no idea what to expect the first time I walked through those aisles filled with porn and glass pipes until I got to the back of the store, to what was called the "glory holes."

I had visited these stores before to buy pipes and nitrous oxide so that I could get high, but I didn't know people went there for sex. As I passed by the stuff that most college guys were there for (pipes, nitrous, and lube), my goal became clear to everyone in the store.

Lurking men, waiting for other interested men to come in, crept behind the shelves of porn. I felt them eyeing me up and down. The man behind the counter smiled and said "Have fun" as I walked briskly by with my head hanging low. The men in the porn aisles began creeping toward the back of the shop like a school of sharks smelling fresh blood. It made the hair stand up on my back, and my skin flushed.

I was met with a warm, damp, darkness that would become an all too familiar place for the next few years. I didn't have to scour the worldwide web for strangers anymore or send anyone pictures. All I had to do was walk past the porn and into the dark corridors containing thirty or so booths side by side.

It felt like a house of horrors, like a place every part of me wanted to run from, but every bit of me needed.

The thrill was intense. After the first visit, I left with a wad of cash and a feeling of euphoria. But I knew the euphoria would turn into deplorable thoughts of shame and suicide...unless I quickly got high. So the drug dealer was the first stop I made. There, I would procure whatever opiate was available as long as it could be put into a needle. I would then go to the gas station nearest his house to shoot up.

The feelings of shame and remorse inched toward my prefrontal cortex as I alternated crudely between my foot pushing on the gas and sudden breaking, while I gripped the steering wheel through the few red lights between my dealer's house and the gas station where I could find relief. By the time I got through the door of the gas station, a sense of calm lowered my shoulders. I knew that within minutes, I would be free—from the guilt, the pain, myself, and anyone who thought anything good or bad about me.

I would fill a little cup with hot water from an area next to the soda machine and stroll across the sticky tile floor into the single use bathroom. For the next ten minutes, that room would be my heaven. I'd sit on the toilet seat and rig up my needle, filling it with dope and hot water. Then, I would look at the contents, and my heart would beat like an estranged lover back in contact after years of separation. I would caress the liquid with my eyes and give up everything for my love.

The needle slid into my arm, carefully and slowly, under the flickering florescent lights of the grungy bathroom. I relished the pinch of the needle. Then, I would say to myself, "if it kills me this time, so be it."

My eyes would roll back, my face would tingle, and my muscles would go numb. I'd sit there without a thought in my head. When I came to, I'd repeat the process once or twice until I had enough in my system to drive home emotion-free.

Eventually, I started to frequent the porn booths even when I didn't need money. I'd go simply for the emotional release and the thrill it offered me. Plus, it was the furthest away from intimacy that I could get while still having sex.

But it was also a place that destroyed any remaining positive view of myself and confirmed all the negative ones I'd carried since childhood. I was no longer confused about my sexuality because I expressed it regularly. I had become a prostitute and liked it. It also meant I didn't need a girlfriend, and I didn't need a job.

I would have moments of clarity after a particularly brutal or gut-wrenching scene in those booths, like a group of men who played out rape fantasies on me. I would have nightmares about them, and all I could do was wake up, shoot up, and drink copious amounts of alcohol until the memories faded.

It's still a wonder how I never contracted any venereal diseases during this time. Maybe it was because I was in Montana. Most guys there protected themselves, but I still believe someone higher up was looking out for me.

Disease or not, this style of living was hardly sustainable for anyone with a soul, and when my soul made an occasional appearance, I ended up feeling horrified and disgusted with myself. Then, I'd do ordinary things for a short time like go on dates with girls and go to concerts with friends. Often, I was barely able to speak because I was so loaded, but at least I felt somewhat like a normal human being.

I just had to keep using drugs despite the repeated consequences. And those consequences got worse. During my senior year of college, I was in hiding. There were two different dealers (a pot dealer and a heroin dealer) looking for me on every corner. So I tucked myself away in the library, and somehow, despite my intense drug use and prostitution, I managed to study my way through college.

NINETEEN

DAMN DOG

I was dope sick and drunk at 10:00 a.m., walking my dog and thinking I would either kill myself or drink until I passed out. My big black dog galloped away from me toward three girls who were sunbathing and giggling on the manicured campus lawn. I think he just had to get away from my negativity, but I walked over to grab him and take him home.

The girls, looking bright and healthy, were overjoyed by the presence of this big dog who still acted like a loving puppy.

"Sorry about the dog," I said with my head held low and a beanie pushing my hair over my eyes.

"No worries!" they all chuckled at the same time.

"Hey, I think I know you," one of the girls said. She had long dark hair and long fair-skinned legs that made me lift my head.

"That's cool," I said flatly, trying to avoid further conversation.

"Oh, yeah!" she exclaimed, holding my dog and petting him while I reached toward him to regain control.

"Psych 100," she continued. "You're one of the proctors for the class."

An opportunity to feel better had just presented itself. If she recognized me, she must have been attracted to me. If she was attracted to me, and I was her proctor, she would probably have sex with me and validate me. I pursued the possibility.

Momentarily shrugging off my withdrawal and grim outlook on life, I opened my eyes big and looked at her with yearning, confidence, and strength.

"Yeah, I sure am. I recognize you, too. I've watched you walk out of the classroom and wanted to chat a couple of times. Being a proctor is hard, though. I'm not supposed to hit on you."

She grinned and turned her head to the side while the other two girls giggled.

"No way," she said, blushing.

"Yeah, totally," I answered with complete confidence. "Here, let me have your phone number, and I'll text you. That way, if you ever need some help, you can contact me."

"Oh, yeah? You're gonna be her tutor?!?" one of her friends suggested.

"Oh, I'll be more than that!" I said as I straightened up with my dog finally back on the leash. I smiled at her, and she smiled back while giving me her phone number. Her name was Callie.

"I'll text you soon. Can't wait to get to know you."

Once we started going out, Callie's presence helped me feel better about myself and avoid my shame. After all, a young girl with minimal experience was looking up to me.

I stopped going to the porn shops and stopped prostituting online. Instead, I spent all of my time with Callie. Besides the drugs, we had a lot of fun with each other. We both enjoyed the outdoors, and we loved talking about philosophy and psychology. And we both enjoyed sex. We did plenty of all of those things.

Then, of course, the shit hit the fan.

When you're an addict and shit hits the fan, there's really only one solution, and it isn't one made with a clear head. So rather than digging out, I began to dig deeper and harder. Things got nasty for this addict right when we found out that our unprotected sex had a consequence.

Callie reacted exactly the opposite. She went sober and began loving me in ways that threatened my depressing view of myself. For the next couple of months, as our baby grew inside of her, I wrestled with demons. I went back and forth to the porno booths, my drug dealer's house, and basements with needles on the ground. I wanted to be anywhere besides home—the place that was yearning for my intimacy.

I was fairly used to things crumbling from my own doing. If life was a Jenga game, I made sure to pull the pieces that would cause the quickest collapse. Not only was I making risky sexual decisions and drug decisions, I was also making risky moves with other people's money.

I was juggling thousands of dollars back and forth between a handful of dealers. One day, I'd be in the favor of one of them, and the next day, I wouldn't have his money and would end up on his hit list. The day after that, I'd take money from another deal to pay someone else off. I was constantly shuffling between debts and dealers.

At that point, any involvement with me had become quite dangerous. But I wasn't about to explain that to a person willing to make me feel like the strong, successful, straight, and able man I pretended and wanted to be. Therefore, I used my uncanny ability to lie and manipulate Callie into marrying me.

Inevitably, my drug life caught up to me. One of the dealers saw us at a concert. A couple of his goons ripped off her shirt and grabbed our arms. I was able to wiggle us free and get lost in the crowd, but I knew the drama was far from done.

We ran out of the concert hall and down the street to our home, where I told Callie to hide under our car that was parked on the street. I went inside to grab my gun and money, and we were going to leave town immediately.

But by the time I got my stuff together, eight guys had surrounded the house. The last thing I had to grab was the gun from my other car. I opened the door and while reaching for the gun, I felt a huge whack deep down my spine that sent me to the ground. I winced in pain, but the adrenaline began coursing through me. So I popped up just like nothing had happened and swung my gun around, clocking one of the intruders in the eye with the barrel. He fell to the ground, but in the next moment, I was slugged across the head and found myself lying next to him while the rest of the men kicked me with all of their strength.

I fought to get up by grabbing onto one of the assailants' legs, wrestling him to the ground. Unfortunately, he got hold of my gun. We both had our hands on the weapon, and I some-how wedged my finger under the trigger, which prevented the gun from going off into my stomach. I could feel my knuckle cracking from the pressure and blood seeping down my arm from the wound inflicted by the trigger. I knew I couldn't hold that position for long, so in one last burst of energy, throwing my legs and arms up through the kicks and punches, I managed to escape.

When my finger was dislodged from the gun, it went off, blasting into the dirt next to me. The echo pulsated between my ears, while the bruises from being kicked countless times in the head added to the ringing deep in my skull. The thugs scattered more quickly than they had come, likely assuming they'd shot me and had, therefore, finished their job.

When the cops arrived, I didn't have much of a story. But luckily, I also didn't have any drugs, money, or guns on me. All of it had been taken. I still had to face Callie, however, because my cover had been blown.

About the same time we had committed to a big wedding with both our families she had began understanding that I was a true and dangerous addict, and there wasn't much I could do to remedy the situation, especially as I was continuing to use heroin every time I went to the bathroom.

TWENTY

First Son

C allie and I packed up our house and moved by the end of the next day. We stayed in the same town, but a little bit outside in a spot secluded enough that it felt safe. We then carried on our everyday life as if nothing had happened. I had promised to stay clean from heroin, and apparently, I pulled off my lies pretty well.

I typically found an excuse to leave first thing in the morning. I'd say I was going to the grocery or to a Narcotics Anonymous meeting, but I'd use the time to find my opioid fix. On most occasions, I'd shoot up in the same old gas station bathroom before heading home.

It was a miserable way to live—leaving my pregnant fiancé first thing in the morning and not returning home until I was faded enough to make it through the day. The next nine months of my two-faced existence hurt Callie to the very core of her being. At that point, since I was mostly on heroin, I was emotionally unavailable.

At least, I hadn't become emotionally abusive ... yet.

I had burned the bridges to a good life in Missoula, where Callie and I met and where I created a dangerous environment to raise a child. So after the baby was born, we figured the best option was to move in with her parents in their small town.

Doing so, however, would have a serious impact on my coping mechanisms. Heroin and other opioids would be virtually nonexistent in a town of 700 people. Leaving Missoula would also mean giving up the porno booths.

My first son was born only a few weeks after the incident with the drug dealers. My life changed forever, but not in the way the typical story goes. Most men straighten up after they hold their child. Not me.

Instead, I just had another thing in my life that made me feel guilty about the way I was living. His presence contributed to my shame. When I held my son in my arms, I melted, and I tried so hard to get clean for him. But without the drugs, I would slip into suicidal thoughts and overwhelming anxiety. I had too many lies and too much shame coating all of those lies. But I really did try very hard.

Unfortunately, my attempts were like Sisyphus: I'd roll up my sleeves and push hard against my addiction, only for it to come crashing down on me again. Unable to clean up for something you love so dearly is an indescribably horrible feeling.

To help my addiction, a doctor gave me Suboxone, an opioid agonist that eases the pain of withdrawal. It put me on what felt like a soft pink cloud. Nothing was great, and nothing was horrible. But on Suboxone, everything was *okay*. It's a perfect drug for addicts if they're willing to seek help while they take it.

But in my case, all I wanted was the drugs. So with time, the inevitable happened. I was unable to get high enough to deal with the added pressure of family life. To compensate, I started taking copious amounts of Benzos, mostly Xanax, and I started drinking heavily. King Alcohol took the throne, driving anyone away who tried to come near. With seething words of cruelty, he assured me that I could find my way back to complete isolation.

I drank from sun up to sun down. If we ever needed anything from the store, I was the first to hop up, put on my shoes, and crank up my engine. If I was smooth and quick enough, I could pop into the liquor store for some mini bottles and grab a forty-ounce beer from the grocery, while also getting what we needed for dinner. I went on errands all the time. Sometimes, I'd purposely forget something from the grocery list just so that I could make another round.

I ended up buying a pair of cowboy boots one day because I was tired of not having a place to stash my mini vodka bottles while driving. That way, I didn't have to make excuses to go to the basement when I needed a drink. I could fit four to six bottles in each boot.

At the time, I was employed as a liftie on the ski mountain in Whitefish, Montana. It was the perfect job for me. I had become a very skilled closet drinker, and doing it while bundled up on a ski mountain was no problem. I was able to drink all day, hiding bottles in my ski jacket while I helped people on the lift.

I'd then go home, sometimes with enough energy to play with my son and put him to bed. Other times, I didn't have enough energy to save face, and I'd become angry, throwing fits that scared both Callie and my one-year-old son, River.

One day, while Callie was working a parade in Whitefish, I strapped River to my back and took him out to meet her there. With my son on my back in a top-heavy baby carrier, I looked more like a straw man on stilts.

I was so drunk that I staggered down the street. The unsure footing of a drunk on ice-covered pathways combined with a crying baby was a recipe for disaster. Callie found us, fallen down and unable to get up. I was too drunk to explain myself, not that there was any explaining required. She took the baby, providing him the safety he deserved.

I, on the other hand, went to the bar.

Later that evening, I came home with a fearful blood alcohol level. Callie said she would be leaving the next day, and in a fit of anger, I threw a trash can through our glass front door and then fell asleep on the ground.

Around 7:30 the next morning, I woke up, checking myself for blood. Luckily, I was in the clear. I had no idea what had happened the night before. Work started at 8:00, so I loaded up my jacket with booze and drove to my post on the ski mountain.

I was able to stay pleasantly drunk through the work day, with jovial spirits coursing through my blood. I went back home for a pleasant evening with my little family. *I loved them so much.* But when I pulled up to the house, Callie's parents' suburban was in my parking spot.

I was actually excited to see my in-laws. Then, as I walked toward the house, I saw the broken window. *Hmm…I wonder how that happened.*

Next, I heard a car door shut behind me. Spinning my body around like a top, I turned to see my wife standing beside the parked suburban. Everyone was sitting inside, loaded up like they were all going out to dinner. *How fun!*

"Mark," she said, "I've already loaded up the baby and packed all my belongings. We're leaving."

"Where are you going?"

"I told you last night after you smashed the window and endangered our son at the parade that my parents were coming to get me."

"Wait…I don't remember any of that. Can we talk about it inside?" I felt a great pang of dread and guilt. All eyes were glaring at me.

"No, you can say bye out here. We're leaving now." She turned and opened the door to sit in the seat next to my son, allowing me space to give him a kiss. He was tightly snuggled into his car seat, and he smiled innocently when he made eye contact with me.

A warm tingle was beginning to rise up in my blood, a sign that I needed a drink soon, or I would start shaking. My priority shifted focus.

"Screw it, I'm going inside. We need to talk about this," I said, but all I wanted was a beer to settle my nerves.

I walked through the broken glass and into the kitchen, where I poured a shot of vodka straight into my mouth and popped open a beer. I turned to go back outside and discuss the matter at hand, but all I saw was an empty parking spot. My wife and son were gone, and I never even said goodbye.

Still, all I could really think about was getting another drink. I felt nothing except the desire to drink heavily. So I did.

For the next two months.

TWENTY-ONE

TAKE ME TO THE RIVER

U pon learning of my drinking habit, the ski mountain fired me. I had become a liability and was constantly calling in sick because I was too drunk by 8:00 a.m. to make my shift. Life got even darker and sadder.

I cried for hours on end. Then, I gagged because the booze choked me when it mixed with the snot that drained into my throat.

As I faced the reality of the separation from Callie and River, I slipped into a deep depression. I couldn't get out of bed. But that meant I didn't have the money to keep drinking, so I began to search for a job.

I managed to get one as a raft guide, but this required training, which was a two-week intensive program. We would practically live on a raft in the river with no booze. I didn't know if it was possible, but I gave it a shot.

It was a wild and scenic river in Glacier National Park. At the beginning of the year, since the river isn't maintained by a dam, the spring runoff creates a thrilling, intense ride. Paddling our clients through waves that could crunch the raft like a toy and send every soul into deadly rapids was enough to take my mind off things. I made it about a month booze-free—until it all became monotonous.

As the river dried up and the thrill slowed down, the raft trips got longer and became drudgery. I had plenty of time to think between rapids, and that time in my head got the best of me. So I started bringing whiskey on board and lived pleasantly drunk. Then ... I hurt my back. While not paying attention, my raft hit a rock, dumping my patrons into the rapids. I pulled everyone in, but I strained my lumbar spine in the process.

When I got home, I propped my legs up and knew I was going to need to take a few days off so that I could heal. I went into my cupboard for some ibuprofen, but before I took the pills, I had a better idea. This was a perfect excuse to get something stronger. It had been a long time, and life wasn't going particularly well. I might as well call an opioid dealer and get high again.

It had been a little over a year, but the dealer I called was still selling. I bought as many as he was willing to sell me, and for the next few days, I got high as a kite. Within a few days, I was shooting heroin again.

As the end of the raft season approached, I stopped showing up to work. Instead, I spent my time either searching for drugs or lying in bed with the needle in my arm. When the drug wasn't available, I resorted to sex. My house transformed from a place with toys and toddler laughter to a dark, rank abyss with trash, empty bottles, drugs, and used condoms.

I began opening my doors to any man who wanted to use me, and there were plenty. I was in good physical shape after my summer of rafting, and I was never hungry when I was on dope. So men from Craigslist and Grindr were always willing.

I'd close my eyes while they did whatever they wanted, and as soon as one would leave, another one was waiting. Some mornings, four or five guys in a row would use me. In between each of them, I drank as I waited, hoping the drugs would arrive.

Usually, by noon, my drug dealer would have more opiates, or I would be drunk enough and sexually used up enough to feel somewhat valued and alive. If I did get some drugs, they would take me into oblivion until the next morning. It was a vicious cycle.

Then, my mother called to say they'd bought a jeep in Montana. Would I want to drive it to Atlanta for them? I didn't have much going for me, so I loaded up the jeep with my opiates, a few big bottles of whiskey and vodka, a trunk full of beer, and a glove box full of weed that I'd smoke and sell in Georgia.

I pulled out of my driveway in Montana first thing in the morning and pulled into my parents' driveway in Atlanta a few days later. I had been blacked out drunk the entire trip.

I have little memory of the trip. Was it fun? I wish I could tell you.

I do recall having sex with a stranger in the back of the jeep one morning. I was also told by some friends later that I stopped in a bar in Louisville, Kentucky and drank with them until 5:00 in the morning. Otherwise, the forty-two-hour car ride is a blur.

But I have a crystal clear memory of the events that followed. When I got to Atlanta, my eyes were bloodshot, and my speech was slurred as I gave my mom a drunken hug. All the empty booze bottles were tossed in the back of the jeep, and the carpet was scorched by cigarette butts.

"Would you like to go to rehab?" Mom asked me.

"No," I answered.

A few days later, after I had recovered from the drive, Mom bought me a plane ticket home and let me know that if I changed my mind, she would pay for rehab. I hugged her and accepted the plane ticket. I needed to get back to my dungeon. I had run out of opioids, so I was becoming dope sick. Withdrawal would settle in soon.

The night I got home was like every other night. I got off the plane, found my drugs, got my booze, closed my blinds, and hit the dark confines of the house. I cranked up the music and had a party with myself. When I took my last shot of black tar heroin into my veins, I felt on top of the world, where I'd stay until morning.

The next a.m., however, I didn't roll around as usual. With that last shot of tar, I had overdosed. I was found in a hammock on my back porch, where I had lay swinging through the cold fall Montana night as the moonlight slid across the sky. I woke up to my friend punching me in the face. She said my lips were purple, and I wouldn't wake up. It was below freezing outside, and I was just wearing a t-shirt and pajama bottoms. By the time I came to, my friend was crying. She thought she'd lost me.

When a fellow addict tells you that you should get help, it's high time to listen. So I picked up my phone and called my mom.

"I'm ready."

My mother called me back within ten minutes and said I was booked to start rehab in Minneapolis. I had a seat on the next plane. In a matter of hours, I was at Hazelden, a counseling hub and one of the leading manufacturers of sobriety literature. It was the place where Eric Clapton got clean.

Before I left for the airport, my friend and I got high one last time and went to the liquor store for my "last" bottle of whiskey.

By the time we got to the airport, I had emptied the bottle into my body. I managed to check in and make it past security. *Miracles never cease.*

I boarded the plane and began pulling out my pill bottles. I surely wouldn't be allowed to have my anxiety meds and Adderall in rehab, so I would have to take most of them. I hid the pills I couldn't take in the soles of my shoes.

By that point, my tolerance for drugs and booze was a tragically well-built fortress. Plus, I really didn't care if I overdosed on the plane. I hated life. But if I lived through the plane flight, maybe I would get clean in rehab, and Callie would come back into my life with my son. Maybe my life *could* get better.

I ordered a few double whiskey gingers to wash the pills down, and by the time we landed in Minneapolis, I couldn't walk. They used a wheelchair to take me off the plane and shuttle me to the rehab center. I have no recollection of anything until the next morning.

I had been wise to hide some of my pills in my shoes because upon awakening, the withdrawal and panic had set in. The nightmare of all nightmares was coming down on me. I was in rehab and would have to face my demons. But those demons would wait because I had enough pills in my shoes to get me through the first couple of weeks.

It's a shame that I faked my way through parts of this rehab because it was such a fine facility. Despite my fakery while I had my stash of pills, I got clean from Xanax within two weeks. (I still missed them, though.) After four days of heavy withdrawal at Hazelden and a month of psychotherapeutic treatment and addiction groups non-stop, I was off opioids and didn't want to go back to that pain. Booze wasn't far behind.

Knowing I had a problem with men, I made it a goal in rehab to concentrate on women and women alone. But Hazelden is a tight community, so conversations between men and women were limited to a couple of words at a time. Regardless, I was somehow able to woo two different girls during the month I was there.

Being with the two girls validated me enough, so I also felt like I had cured my gay and was finally straight. Lies to myself had become just as powerful as lies to other people.

In the fall, upon graduating from rehab for heroin addiction, I sought refuge to rebuild my life in a sober house in Loveland, Colorado. Putting down heroin meant I needed to relearn everything about life. Therefore, I went to two or three sober groups a day—trying desperately to figure out how sober and clean people did things like wake up in the morning, talk to friends, go to work—you know, the normal stuff.

I began working evenings as a cook at a Cajun restaurant that had the best shrimp and grits west of the Mississippi, and I slowly learned how to navigate my daily life.

While in rehab, I decided it was imperative to my sobriety to meet other sober men and bond with them through outdoor activities. Normal people had normal friends, not just friends who got high with them. Mountain biking, hiking, rock climbing, skiing, and rafting—anything outside with an element of thrill or adventure was necessary for me to feel connected to the universe, grateful for nature, and disconnected from my addiction. I knew this would be a challenge because historically, with other men, I only had drug relationships, unemotional sexual trysts, or friendships in which I stole their identity to create my own. In short, I was still a mess.

TWENTY-TWO

ANOTHER RYAN

Always in sweatpants at the sober meetings, he was tall, funny, and athletic with long, dark, wavy hair. All I really wanted was a platonic friendship, but he was so beautiful. And the way he talked in meetings set a fire on top of my shoulders where my head should be. Coincidentally, his name was Ryan.

His laid-back approach to life intrigued me, and his smile all the more. Finally, I decided to introduce myself—the first step toward intimacy. His hair swung to the side as he glanced over at me. I felt small and caught, like I had just jumped from a precipice, but a strong wind lifted me back up.

"H...hi. Hi," I stammered. "I just wanted to say I've liked what you had to say on multiple occasions."

"Aww, thanks," he responded, reaching out his hand. "I'm Ryan."

"Nice to meet you, Ryan," I said as I grabbed his hand. His shake was firm, and he met me with unmistakable eye contact that made me feel noticed. I grew a little from my otherwise small vision of myself.

"I'm Mark," I replied, puffing my chest out a little more.

"Well, Mark, I've liked your shares, too. I have to say, you have a poetic way of delivering your insight, and I really enjoy listening."

I blushed a bit, and my lips spread on their own to show the signs of a tense smile. "I write a lot of poetry. I love poetry."

"I can tell," he said.

"Ya . . . ya . . . wouldn't wanna meet up sometime, would you? You know, for a cup of coffee?" A moment of silence came over us, and before he could even answer, I came up with an excuse for asking the question so soon. "It's just, I've been here a few weeks and haven't met another guy I can relate to. From all your shares and the way you hold yourself, I feel like we would have something in common."

"Oh, sure; I'd love that," he said.

Tending to want everything to happen in the moment, I replied, "Awesome! What are you doing now?"

He laughed. "I've gotta work at the restaurant until 11:00 tonight. So how about tomorrow at 2:00 p.m.?"

"Perfect," I said as we walked toward the door.

I grabbed my long board that was resting on the wall and opened the door for him. As a southern boy, I knew to open doors for girls, but what do you do for a guy you're crushing on? I felt awkward. He smiled at me as he walked through, ducking his head slightly as if the door frame was short, but it wasn't. It clearly felt a little awkward for him, too.

"You ride that thing everywhere, don't you?"

"Yeah, man, I love my long board. The weather here in Loveland is perfect for it. Not too hot. Not too cold. And if it snows, it's gone from the street in like an hour, which is so different from where I'm from in Montana."

"Oh, man, Montana," he muttered, sounding excited. "I can't wait to chat. Being from Montana, you probably love the mountains, right?"

"Well, sure, yes. I mean, that's part of the reason I chose Loveland for my sober house."

"Awesome. Then, it sounds like we have a lot to talk about!"

What did he mean? Did he know I was gay? Would I tell him? I could feel that he was watching as I got on my long board and made my way down the street, and I wanted to look cool. I made it to the first street and abruptly turned so that I could get out of view, pressure gone.

But then, I started thinking. *What if he's gay? Should I avoid him? Maybe I shouldn't even meet him. No, I can't continue to walk around in fear of my secrets. I've got to at least meet him.*

Sober programs are pretty straightforward about secrets: they can be dangerous. I'm not supposed to keep them, but I'm definitely not supposed to walk in fear of them because they can cause me to want to drink. Historically, for me, this had been very much the case. So would I tell Ryan my secret? I had no idea. All I could think about at that point was our coffee meeting the next afternoon.

After collecting my thoughts and nursing my fears, I made a huge leap in self-acceptance. If I was this jittery over coffee with a cute guy, it was clear my homosexuality wasn't cured. I decided it was time to try coming out, although I wasn't going to tell everyone. I decided I might even keep it a secret from Ryan, but I was definitely going to tell my roommate.

"Uh…Laura, do you think I can tell you something?"

"Sure, Mark. What is it?" she replied casually while putting away the dishes. The loud clinking noises flustered me. I needed full attention to say something this landmark to another person. She was also sober and had been working the program. So I knew if I phrased it like a sober group confession, she would sit down and take me seriously.

"I just have something to say that I've hardly told anyone before, and I'd like you to be the first person in my life now that I share it with. But you must not tell anyone. Is that okay?"

"Oh…oh!" she perked up and sounded excited. "Are you telling me something because your sponsor said to share secrets with a closed-mouth friend?" she paused and came closer, leaning toward me. "Mark, am I lucky enough to be your closed-mouth friend?"

Too nervous to make a joke out of it, I just replied, "Sure, but please, you really do have to remain closed-mouthed about it!"

"Of course!" she jumped back as if shocked I'd question her fortitude against gossip.

"Okay, okay," I said and continued, trying not to stutter. "I just think that as my roommate, you should know something about me." Her face didn't flinch. If you spend enough time in sober programs, you learn some pretty shocking things, and after a while, they lose their effect on you.

She could tell it was very hard for me. "Mark, you can trust me. I promise. You don't have to worry."

"Okay, ergh, my palms are sweaty!" I diverted attention and let out a little laugh. "So I just needed to tell you this because you're my roommate, and I want to make sure you're okay with me being here after you know,"

"Mark, Jesus, it'll be fine," she said, frustrated. Then, she made a slight joke, "I mean unless you're like a murderer or something." We both smiled, but neither of us laughed because this was obviously a serious matter.

I was still uncomfortable even saying the word "gay" out loud.

"Well, so … since I was a young boy, I've been a little confused. I think I'm … *bi*." I watched Laura intently for an expression.

"Is that it?! Oh, my gosh! Why were you so nervous? I think that's awesome!"

Saying "I think I'm bi" when I knew I was gay was like saying "I think I'm lactose intolerant" while throwing up after every glass of milk. I hadn't even taken ownership of the preference. My confession was incomplete, so I didn't feel relieved. But it would have to do for the time being.

"And I have a crush on a guy who may come over. His name is Ryan."

I was excited to meet Ryan at the coffee shop the next day. My crush was bubbling up inside, but I wasn't going to hit on him. I truly wanted to make a male friend—an authentic one whose identity I wasn't going to rob.

When we met, I was still shooting to appear straight because I didn't know if he was gay. My intentions were all in the right place.

I arrived early, as I often do because of my anxious nature. I checked my phone religiously until he arrived. I acted at first like I didn't see him so as to avoid exposing my excitement. He walked up to me, cool as a cucumber, and joined me on the next bar stool. We sat around the shaky table with louder than comfortable music intruding on our space.

Our initial conversation went well enough that we arranged to take the next step with a hike together. That would get us out of the loud, congested, distracting city so that we could truly get to know one another.

As usual, I felt scared on my way to pick him up for our hike. I was afraid of divulging information, getting close, and becoming more vulnerable. When you live in the city, going on a hike is a full-day affair. I had to be willing to have a day-long conversation with another man, most of which would be in the small confines of my car. I tried to play it cool, but without drugs or booze, that was unnatural for me. It was intolerably uncomfortable.

Usually, when faced with the need for such conversation, I would discuss small things like the weather and the flora of the surrounding landscape. I'd talk about politics, sports, cars, or my favorite subject, drugs. On the way to the trailhead, I discussed anything and everything with Ryan to keep from any intimate topics.

Outside the car, the climate changed drastically as we climbed higher into the mountains bordering Rocky Mountain National Park. By the time we drove through the gates of the park, snow clung to the surrounding forest bed, and we laughed about our lack of preparedness. Our shared laughter brought us closer, which meant more uncomfortable vulnerability for me.

I parked my little black SUV at the trailhead, and we began walking through the knee-deep snow. Ryan wore his usual tennis shoes and sweatpants, while I trekked along slightly more prepared in my boots. We were mostly quiet as we hiked. The beauty of the place was awe-inspiring. Mountains tore through the horizon like knives tearing away at the seams of a blanket. The contrast of the black and white made the jagged summits look otherworldly as they towered above our heads.

It was so cold, and we were so unprepared that after no more than a mile, we headed back to the refuge of the car. We hopped in and began warming the engine and our bones. As I rubbed my hands together while twisting my head side to side to toss the snow out of my shaggy hair, Ryan reached across the center console toward my leg. With the same firm grip he used during our handshake, he began to caress me.

I stopped shaking my head and looked toward him. "I'm so glad we did this," he said. "I've lived here a few months and have yet to meet a guy."

Somehow, my willingness to hike had been misread. I wasn't looking for a guy, and I didn't think I even put out that vibe. In fact, upon leaving rehab, I had made a celibacy pact to abstain from women and men for six months in order to avoid becoming distracted from my rehabilitation.

My fear bubbled up like an overflowing pot of boiling water, taking me back to childhood. Unable to cope with the fear, I reverted to that little boy who had once enjoyed playing the part of the little girl, even though I knew it was wrong. I became giddy, and we drove home talking about how excited we were to have met someone.

The next thing I knew, we were planning our next rendezvous. But this time, we wanted a little more privacy. Neither of us was willing to wait too long, so a few hours later, after he had a chance to go home and run some errands, Ryan came over to my house.

Starting a movie was silly, but we did it anyway, out of habit. The next thing I knew, our bodies were entangled in heat as I took him into me with my teeth clenched and my eyes pinched closed, contracting every muscle in my face. But soon, the pain was over, and euphoria set in.

Sex is a powerful drug. It can eradicate fear and shame, making you feel whole and complete, at least temporarily.

Nevertheless, I awoke the next day in a dreadful cloud of shame, while also holding a contradictory smug smile of pleasure. Because I had learned in rehab that it was important to be honest if you wanted sobriety, I knew I had to tell him I was trying not to be interested in men, at least romantically.

I rubbed my eyes through the film of regret that coated my vision and lugubriously rolled over my feather-filled comforter, dropping my feet off the side of the bed onto the shag carpet. I walked to the dresser where my cell phone was charging, ready to give him the dreaded call. To my surprise there was already a text from him:

"I have HIV."

That bombshell set fire to every cell in my body. My fear reached the same height I experienced as a child when I asked my mother about AIDS. The worst fear of my childhood.

Screw the sober living situation. I called my doctor to request a refill on my Xanax prescription. He denied me, so I headed straight to the closest recreational marijuana store. I felt a surge of relief from the smell alone. I asked the pleasant gentleman behind the counter for their strongest Indica, telling him I was having trouble with sleep and anxiety. I then walked out with a bag full of Kush, Cheba Chew edibles, a sucker, and a new glass pipe. Before I got to my car, I ate an edible and popped the sucker in my mouth. Then, I loaded a glass pipe and smoked my way toward oblivion and toward a hospital, where I would find a way to get Xanax.

I went to the emergency room to see a doctor so that I could achieve two things. First, I needed to know if I had HIV.

Second, and more importantly at that point, I needed to refill my prescription for Xanax. Unfortunately, they didn't do STD testing, but I did get to leave with a small prescription.

Then, I went to the next hospital. They didn't do STD testing either. I went to two other emergency rooms, increasing my medical debt ten-fold (a debt that took me four years to pay off). I found out I'd have to wait weeks to know if I got HIV from Ryan.

During those ensuing weeks, I ate Xanax like candy and smoked hundreds of dollars' worth of weed, blowing the smoke out of the bathroom window of my sober living home.

Once high, I proceeded to harm the people who harmed me. First up was my new lover, Ryan. The interesting pattern of fear related to intimacy and vulnerability was that I first harmed the people I had grown to love the most. I came up with any excuse to hurt them that justified my behavior. I had an excuse this time for sure—an HIV scare.

Looking back, though, I realize that the HIV scare wasn't why I was angry. What upset me the most was how it could expose my secret.

I left Ryan voicemails filled with verbal daggers so sharp that they could have brought down a brick wall. I did everything I could to tear into his soul. The result? Silence. I never heard from him again. I heard from others, though, that he suffered a similar fate as me—relapse.

I received the test results that I didn't have HIV, but that brought me no closure and very little satisfaction. It wasn't HIV that I was scared of—it was coming out that terrified me. And I had to get as far away from the place that knew my secret.

So it wasn't long before my bags were packed for Montana.

Sitting next to me in the passenger seat was a gallon jug of vodka to keep me company during the ride. I left Colorado behind, as well as any notion of sobriety. I gave up, choosing relapse and choosing to hate the person I had gotten close to.

TWENTY-THREE

A BREAK AND A VOID

I stayed high and drunk for a long time, gaining a lot of weight in both my gut and my soul. Nevertheless, after Callie formally divorced me, I managed to get off heroin.

I started working a stellar job as a program manager for the severely mentally ill at a clinic in Montana. After I'd remained clean from heroin for two years, I got promoted. It was the first promotion I had ever achieved, and I was on cloud nine. Everything was going well for me.

Well, everything but my drinking.

My excuse was that counseling was a taxing job. So every day after work, I went straight to a wildly unpopular bar and ordered two Long Island iced teas. I drank them while I filled my client charts for the day. After the heavy stuff hit my veins, I either had a few beers at the bar or headed home where I'd pop a few pills, smoke a joint, and drink some more. Either way, bar or home, I kept drinking all night until I passed out.

Unbelievably, work was going well in spite of this. My clients liked me, and I liked them. I made some great friends at work, and for the first time in my adult life, I was invited to trivia nights, birthday parties, and barbeque get-togethers. It was amazing. I felt like I had found my tribe.

I walked through the office, giving and receiving high fives, good mornings, smiles, and pats on the back. I joked with colleagues while the crappy office coffee brewed. I not only felt a part of something, but I felt *useful*. Every day, I was helping people who needed my help.

But life can change in an instant.

On a winter night that was just blustery enough to debate between a heavy jacket or something lighter, I discovered I was fine in my thick white and red flannel that looked like it came off of Paul Bunyon's back. I was on my way to a going away party for someone who had become quite special.

Her name was Taylor, a jovial, loud, heavyset, exciting bundle of fun. I loved spending time with her. She was rambunctious and cracked jokes that could take the monkey off anyone's back. She was always available for a big ol' hug on the hard days. With my arms spread as wide as possible, I wasn't able to wrap her all in, but I tried anyway. I loved hugging her. It made me feel warm and cared for. She seemed to have a mother's heart.

At the same time, she was who she was, and if you had a problem with it, you had best move aside. Sometimes, you could tell the laughter she provoked from others was actually fear.

I received my promotion largely because Taylor was leaving, and I was set to fill her shoes. This would be impossible, of course. She was like the "big mamma" of the center.

The party would consist of dinner followed by karaoke. Then, I was to spend the night at my buddy's house since he lived just down the street from the karaoke bar. Not having to drive after the party was a celebration in and of itself. So I went wild. I skipped eating and drank everything. I'm sure I sang "Five to One" by The Doors so I could hiss like a possessed snake through my drunken lips.

I vaguely remember walking to my buddy's house with a few other people, including Taylor. I always loved it when a party continued at someone's home. All of a sudden, it was freedom. We could do what we wanted without the threat of being kicked out of the bar. So upon walking through the door, I whipped out my pills. I crushed some, snorted them, and handed out a few.

"What are they?" Taylor asked.

"Xanax."

"Oh, hell, no. I'm not taking those while I'm drinking!"

"Suit yourself!" I slurred back in a louder than necessary voice to match her objection.

Xanax has long been known to be a dangerous drug to mix with alcohol. It causes not just loss of judgment, but also severe memory loss. It amplifies the effects of alcohol to the point of oblivion, which was my goal every night. And I usually achieved it.

That night would be no different in that respect. I was good at partying, but I did the same thing whether other people were around or not.

Like most parties, the responsible people went home, and the ones who couldn't drive stayed to eat frozen pizza and sleep strewn about the house like dirty laundry. I was draped over the couch with one leg up and one leg on the floor, like a puppet that had been dropped and discarded.

Then, I felt a tugging. With only one leg on the couch, the tugging pulled me off balance and rattled my disoriented nerves enough to come to…slightly. Before I could react, my cock was in someone's mouth, and they were trying to pull my pants down further to get a better grasp of the whole package.

"Taylor?" I slurred. "Are we really doing this right now?"

"Mmm hmm," her voice gurgled through her lips and saliva. Her speed picked up once she knew I was awake.

I grabbed her head. "What the hell?" I said.

She looked up and smiled wide.

"I've wanted to do this for so long, Mark. You're such a stud, and you get me so wet."

The compliment, along with my inability to take much action, sent my head back toward the pillow. Out cold.

When I woke up again, there was pressure on me. I felt my cock fully supported and warm, and the weight on my torso pushed me down. I opened my eyes again.

"What the fuck!?" I tried to lift Taylor off of me, but she was far too heavy. She had her head back and a hand up her shirt. She seemed to be enjoying herself. I raised my upper body in order to lift her off of me. Successful, I pulled myself back onto the arm of the couch, and with double vision, I stared at her in bewilderment.

Am I being raped? I asked myself.

Taylor crawled toward me and told me it was her first time in a long time. She begged me to continue. I stood up, facing her back as her chest pressed into the couch, and I began to fuck her from behind. I remember doing it fast and hard, humping in raw anger and confusion. Then, it was over, and I fell back asleep on the couch.

When I woke up in the morning, Taylor was gone, and my buddy was making breakfast. He came out of the kitchen when he heard me stirring.

"Dude, how was Taylor?!"

"What do you mean?" I tried to deny it, as I barely remembered it and was trying to chalk it up to a dream.

"I came out to use the bathroom and saw you behind her."

"Oh, my God. I can't believe it. Dude, I didn't want to do that," I exclaimed. "She forced me!"

He laughed a deep belly laugh. "What do you mean, like she raped you?"

"Yeah, bro! What the fuck? I wouldn't have fucked her."

"Well, I'm sure you just made her year," he said as he walked nonchalantly back into the kitchen.

Terror. Bewilderment. Frustration. Despair. In the alcoholic world, these are known as the hideous four horsemen. The consequences of overindulgence with drugs and alcohol. They all set in, but it wasn't the first time I'd experienced them, of course. And I knew damn well how to deal with those horsemen.

I dusted off my clothes and popped open a beer. I'd need a few more before I could drive home. Yes, I had to be drunk to drive.

Luckily, it was Thursday, so I had Friday, Saturday, and Sunday to drink it off. I didn't sober up at any moment during those days.

When Monday arrived, my conscience was clear, and I was ready to help the men and women at the center. I walked through the hallways giving my normal high fives, and no one talked about the going away party. After all, most of the office personnel had left early enough to miss what happened.

I rounded the corner to my office and saw a printed piece of paper on my desk that had a Black man's face on it. His expression looked as though he had just won a million dollars. It read: "Go ahead. Call the cops. They can't un-rape you."

I grabbed the piece of paper and shoved it into my briefcase, looking hastily around the room to see if anyone else had seen it.

I fell into a panic. The room spun out, and inside my head, the tires screeched and the windows shattered like an inner car crash. Reality lit a fuse in my brain and exploded. It was one thing to *think* I had been raped. It was another altogether to know that the perpetrator felt the same way about it and would shove it in my face.

I walked briskly toward the door, avoiding eye contact with everyone. I made it to my truck and turned on the engine, driving to the closest convenience store, where they sold $8 craft beer singles. I bought two. It was only 9:00 in the morning, but I chugged them in my car.

Then, I went back to work and headed straight for my supervisor's office. He was a nice, young, gay man—the most understanding listener I've ever met. He always maintained eye contact as he pinched his lips, stroked his chin, and nodded—even if the topic was as flippant as a slight change in the barometric pressure. You could tell he valued everyone.

I knocked upon his door.

"One minute," I heard his muffled voice through the door.

If he was with a client, I might not get to talk to him for another hour. There was no way I could wait that long. Taylor could walk down the hallway at any moment like a steamroller. She'd get them all to laugh at me. I'd be like that little boy again in girls' underwear, dancing while Cody snickered and pointed.

By the time my supervisor's door opened, my face was hot, my hands were sweaty, and the alcohol was already wearing off.

"Jay, I have something extremely personal to bring to your attention."

He paused and fixed his eyes on me, assuming his listening position before he even uttered an agreement.

"Okay. What's going on Mark? You seem troubled."

"Troubled? I'm more than troubled. I don't even know how to say this." I really didn't.

"You know how it was Taylor's going away party?" I continued.

"Yeah, that was on Thursday. I heard it ended up being pretty crazy!" he chuckled, dropping back into his chair and letting go of his understanding listening posture.

"Yeah, it was pretty crazy, I guess, but I'm not here to joke about it."

"Well," he leaned forward, looking serious again, "you know what happened there doesn't pertain here, right?"

"I know, Jay, and I didn't want to bring this here. But then I got this on my desk."

I pulled out the paper that had the rape meme on it. He looked at it in confusion. "Someone put this on your desk?"

"Yes."

"What does it even mean?"

"It means that no matter what I do, I can't get away from the fact that..."

I tried to say her name but it didn't come out.

"She raped me."

"Who?"

"She doesn't work here anymore."

"Taylor? No way!"

The disbelief caught me off guard. He didn't understand after all. I moved toward the door and began to walk out.

"I'm going to need to take the rest of the day off, Jay."

I ran out of the office building and got into my truck. Those beers had been good, so I went back to the store to buy a couple more for the drive home.

After a while, I got a phone call and saw "Jay" on the caller ID.

"Mark, I'm sorry. I want to talk more about what happened. It just shocked me," he said.

"I know. It shocked me, too. I understand."

"Can you come back to the office, or are you already in Whitefish?"

"I'm already home. Can we talk tomorrow?"

"Sure. And Mark? I'm here for you. I have put a restriction on Taylor. She can't come back on campus. This is a safe place. Why don't you come in around noon tomorrow while it's quiet, and we can chat?"

"Perfect. Thanks for understanding."

When I entered Jay's office the next day, I found out he'd done some research. He had found out that there was very little he could do since Taylor was no longer an employee. He placed a restriction on the campus and alerted her that if she came onto the property, they would call the police. He then told me about the victim advocate office. It's the place you go when you're a victim of a crime and need help but don't know where to turn. He would take care of my clients while I went there.

I was terrified to go, but I got myself there. When I told the woman at the front desk that I was there to meet with the victim advocate, she looked at me strangely. I only sat in the waiting room for about two minutes before my head filled with steam, and I popped out of my chair and lunged toward the door. Just as I started to pull the fancy copper handle of the heavy wooden courthouse door toward me, I heard a woman behind me say, "Mark? Mark Turnipseed?"

I was caught. I let the door slide back into place, trapping me in the stale courthouse air. I turned and faced a woman with the warm countenance of a child's librarian. She was approachable and comforting in that grandmother-with-a-cookie-and-a-warm-glass-of-tea sort of way. I halfway expected her to have a large bowl of potpourri beside a box full of Wrigley's Doublemint Gum just like my own grandmother.

Her innate sweetness allowed me to easily divulge every little detail of what had happened to me. After spewing my story, she lifted her head from her notebook where she had been watching her fingers scramble to scratch the appropriate words on the page.

When she spoke, she expressed her shock. "In my years as a victim advocate, it's been very rare for a man to say he was raped. But it isn't just that rarity that makes it shocking. It's what happened after that's the most shocking."

Then came the words that made me feel faceless and desperately alone in the world. This exceedingly kind woman said, "If you were a woman, you would have everything you need for complete protection and prosecution. But as a man, if you take this to any court in Montana, there's a 99% chance that you'll be the one who ends up charged with rape."

I don't remember much about what happened after that moment. I know I walked out of the courthouse because I ended up somewhere else. I also know that within a few weeks, I was fired from two jobs within a month. I dumped my then-girl-friend in a fit of anger and suffered a severe concussion while downhill skiing at fifty-five miles per hour.

The doctor told me that if I continued drinking, I might never recover from the concussion. He said I could end up permanently disabled.

So would that finally be my bottom that would lead me to sobriety?

No, I decided I would welcome disability.

I knew someone who made the strongest moonshine known to man. So I drove forty-five minutes to his place in the country, where I procured two gallons in eight tightly sealed mason jars.

On the forty-five-minute drive back home, I began following my new dream.

In order to document my feelings about this portion of my life, I had to get help from a short booklet called *When a Man is Raped: A Survival Guide*. In the portion titled, "common reactions men experience after rape," they say that since most people believe rape only happens to females, men experience increased isolation, feelings of shame, and loss of self. Most men report feeling like they are less of a man because men should be able to defend themselves. They feel disgusted with themselves because they either couldn't or didn't fight back. Most men engage in seriously self-destructive behaviors, often increasing their use/abuse of drugs and alcohol. They become aggressive with their romantic partners, friends, and coworkers, and they tend to isolate themselves from others.

As I write this, I'm still processing my feelings from the experience. I shoved them away into a portion of my closet that you can't see even when the closet is left open and cleared of clutter. These feelings require a crowbar and a key. First, you'd have to lift up the floorboards in the closet and then open a safe that lies deep inside the enclosure.

Childhood trauma made me question a lot of things and was responsible for my peculiar relationship with sexuality. Childhood trauma also affected every relationship I had as an adult.

But when I was raped as an adult, I felt like I lost the last piece of my will to live. And there was no help for me. So I stopped calling friends and didn't answer my phone. I was so far gone that I didn't believe there was a way to feel human again.

Before that experience, I had used prostitution in a strange way to feel worthy, which is almost certainly related to my childhood abuse. After the rape, I didn't even feel I was worthy of prostitution. I ceased exploiting myself on Craigslist and other sites. All I had was Xanax, a great pot dealer who delivered to my house, five hundred hits of LSD, and a couple of gallons of moonshine.

I sold LSD remotely and hid in my psychedelic drunk hole of a house. I kept my windows shut and my music loud. The one social thing I did before my concussion was ski. I could easily make that activity very antisocial by simply skiing faster than any sane person, allowing me to be alone on the slopes.

But I couldn't ski anymore either, so I simply departed from life completely.

Turnipseed Family picture, 1990. Left to right: Benjamin, Stephanie, Cheryl (mother), Mark, Ben (father), Julie

Baseball Sea Island, 7 years old

Mark and Caroline visiting Sea Island in 2006

Mark with Newborn River, 2011. Slipping back into heroin

Mark before sobriety and Mark crossing the Ironman finish line

Mark at the end of his 1st triathlon

Mark with newborn Elliott and 7–year–old River.
Clean and sober 1 year

Mark with Elliott, 2020

Mark with River, 2020

TWENTY-FOUR

MARK, IT'S TIME TO WAKE UP

I lay in bed as the medicine begins to kick in. Upon awakening, I quickly take some pills to bury at least some of my emotions. I toss them back with a swig of vodka from a bottle sitting beside my bed.

After about thirty minutes, I have enough mental and emotional clearance to rise up and meander to the fridge for a beer. I pop it open and walk to the couch that sits in front of a TV that, while not huge, is big enough to help me get lost in whatever pictures it provides while I get high.

My coffee table, which is four feet by three feet, is filled with smoking devices: two bongs, a few pipes, rolling papers, one ash tray for the bongs and pipes, and one ashtray for joint roaches. The rest of the space is taken up by empty beer bottles and Hot Pocket wrappers. I rarely leave my house unless it's for McDonald's and more beer. After getting my supplies, I rush home to get back to my couch.

This is a description of every day in my life after the rape. I woke up and pressed repeat. That was my existence, and it was all I wanted.

At that point, I had enlarged from 170 to 215 pounds in about three months' time. It started to hurt because I spent so much time lying down. But it was nothing that some pot, moonshine, and pills wouldn't remedy.

One day, I was losing myself in an episode of *Criminal Minds*, and I had no idea what day it was. The phone rang at 9:30 a.m., and the caller ID said "Georgia."

I fought with myself over letting it ring or picking it up since it was most likely family. Answering won the battle.

"Mark, it's Dan!" the voice was unmistakable. Jovial and thrilled like a kid getting ready to take a trip to Disney or a tour on a space shuttle, it was the voice of my older cousin.

"Yeah, I knew it was you when you said my name."

"Ha! We haven't talked in forever, so how did you recognize my voice?!"

"Yeah, it's been a long time. What brings you to call me?"

"I'm coming to Montana!"

"Oh, cool."

Plenty of family members had called me and told me they were coming to Montana. But 100% of the time in the twelve years I had been in the state, none had made it the five hours north to Whitefish after visiting my other cousin in Bozeman.

"I'll be landing in a few hours. About to board the plane now!"

Clearly, he had already set things up for his visit in Bozeman. Our cousin there was twenty years my elder and had her life together with a nice house, beautiful family, and loving husband.

She was always an absolute joy to be around ... compared to me. My life was the complete opposite of hers.

"Well, I'll bet they're ready for you in Bozeman. What are ya'll gonna do?"

Ski season had just ended, and Dan wasn't much of an outdoorsman. So I was slightly curious about the nature of his trip.

"I'm coming to Whitefish, buddy!"

My head started to spin, so I took a swig of moonshine. That stuff was so strong that with a simple sip, I could drastically increase my level of drunk.

"What?" I semi-coughed/gagged back.

"Yeah, I decided to come out this morning, so I got a plane ticket!"

"Um ... well, shit. When do you land?"

"Like I said, a few hours!"

I replied with a reluctant and obligatory, "Do you need me to pick you up from the airport?"

"That would be great, Mark. I'll call you when I land."

"Sounds good." Click.

Why on earth was he coming to visit me? I wondered if someone told him about my depression. I knew Dan had recently gotten sober, so maybe someone suggested he pay me a visit. But then again, no one really knew what was going on with me because I didn't have any visitors. I had only talked to my parents a couple of times over the past few months. They had known I had my ski accident, but they didn't know much else.

Nevertheless, all of those questions would have to wait. It was time to get loaded enough to shower and drive to the airport.

Surprisingly, during Dan's visit, we rarely discussed sobriety or our troubles. But I noticed that he had a genuine interest in my life. When I talked, he listened intently and made eye contact with me. This was different from the Dan I knew before sobriety, who always seemed to be waiting for the next joke he could make.

He also seemed to enjoy everything, even the simplest things from chicken wings to a walk in the park. I didn't understand it, but I knew I wanted to feel that way, too.

We did everything together until it was time to fall asleep. He would go to bed, and I would sit on the porch drinking and playing my mandolin until I was able to pass out. He was also gone most mornings by the time I got up and would arrive with coffee shortly after I'd had my first beer. He had found a sober group down the street from my house.

When it was time for him to leave, I wanted to spend every last minute with him before taking him to the airport. So I asked if I could go to the meeting with him. I wouldn't be able to walk the three blocks without a beer in my hand, however, so I drove us there.

That's how I made it to my first sober meeting since leaving Colorado. I went to that same meeting most every morning for the next year. Dan had shown me what was possible, so like him, I desperately wanted to enjoy the ground I was walking on and the air that was filling my lungs. I had seen it work with many others, and I knew I had never given the program an honest effort.

It was clearly written in the program curriculum that for me to work the program honestly, one other person would have to hear all of my secrets. I had tried that with my former roommate, but by telling her I was "bi," I fell short.

I could still barely say the word "gay" out loud in front of people. I was too scared of it and what it meant for my life. So no matter how important it may have been, I was unwilling to tell anyone in the program.

I sat in the meetings, got to know some good people, learned a lot, and even managed to abstain from drinking for a while. But the lack of honesty meant I wasn't much better. All it would take to put me right back in the throes of turmoil was the slightest stressful event.

Even though I was still smoking pot and taking pills, my life became exponentially better once I dropped the bottle. I also began shedding some of the weight I had gained from my booze and poor diet. I believed I would be okay as long as I didn't drink.

I planned to leave Montana after the summer and get a place in Alaska, where I could live quietly and peacefully without having to come out to anyone.

I was in reasonably high spirits, but I hadn't shared laughs with anyone in a long time. I was lonely.

TWENTY-FIVE

AVA & MARK

She stood on the back of a truck with piles of dirt and moldy, wilted, smelly spring undergrowth that's found after snow melts. She had somehow discovered the single blooming flower in all of Montana and had that sucker poking out of her greasy hair, which settled over her shoulders, radiating the sun's light like a golden calf set above thousands as they paid homage.

The torn Carhartt jeans smeared in manure and her sweaty shirt smudged in dark brown Montana mud faded away as her smile and her eyes penetrated me like daggers. I had felt tired, but not after I saw her.

This woman's presence could bring love to a war, conjure rains from a drought, and provide hope to a world slipping off its axis. If she had been trained as a war medic, she could have made the dead not only walk, but run, jump, and slay anything in their way. I'm certain of this, because I know what she did for this wounded man, who saw her on the back of that dirty ass truck.

The saying goes, "Surround yourself with people who bring out the best in you." Ava was one of those people.

In an attempt to build a friendship with her, I transformed my façade into a man with a plan. I clung to the mask of the steady and reliable guy even tighter than my very skin clings to my face.

I was only just finding my footing with sobriety, so I don't know if I was quite ready for the sudden jolt of health, love, and good life that Ava would breathe into me by her mere presence. She not only brought out the best in me, but when I looked in her eyes, I felt as if I were the man I was supposed to be—the one God had created, the son of my parents, and the father of my son.

Once we met, we hit it off quickly. We were connected like two pontoons floating down the same wild river supporting a wonderful boat. Of course, to say we had a few kinks to work out is an understatement, but despite our rocky start, it was apparent that we both wanted to make our love story happen. If it had been put into a movie, ours would have been the most predictable love story ever, plummeting at the box office. There was no surprise for us or our families as to where we were headed.

So just two weeks after our first date, we moved in together. A month later, we tied the knot by having a tattoo artist chisel rings onto our fingers in a dingy studio shop in Kalispell.

Ava had a great deal going for her when our worlds converged. Throughout adulthood, she had been an honest and diligent worker who had saved her money. She had a solid network of colleagues and friends, great job references, an admirable goal with clear steps toward achieving it, and even a tiny house that she had built with her own hands. She was the most self-reliant woman I had ever met.

I was the complete opposite. I had worked eighteen different jobs in a town of 7,000 people. I had made a bed in all three northwest Montana jails. A month before meeting Ava, I was stuck deep into the fabric of my couch like tomato sauce. I had a month's supply of Xanax and $5,000 worth of hash oil within arm's reach. Needless to say, to get this woman to marry me, I had to be a master of disguise.

In order to try to control relationships, I had a habit of doing anything I could to make a woman believe she needed me. But no one likes to live under another person's thumb, so I was used to being slapped and kicked. I was accustomed to dodging glasses and bowls as they were thrown at me.

Still, old habits die hard. So at the end of August, when the smoke in the mountains of Montana became thick, I used the environmental disaster as an opportunity. Since Ava lived off the grid in a tiny house tucked in the woods, I attempted to act as a source of life support in our time of smoky tragedy by suggesting we move in together.

Later, Ava admitted that she took the suggestion as an insult, reluctantly dragging her feet into my city home. Nevertheless, we moved into my family's small ski cabin in Whitefish and began to craft our life together.

Since I had put down the bottle, my late nights ceased, and my early morning ritual became my thriving point. I was always asleep around 6:30 or 7:00 p.m. because I was smoking so much pot that my drug dealer could have afforded to drop every other client. I was also popping Xanax as if they were coming out of a never-ending Pez dispenser. Somehow, I believed this was a good stab at sobriety.

I would wake up around 5:00 a.m., do some yoga, and walk the two blocks down the street to the small-town sober meeting.

I was still incapable of telling the truth, so before Ava moved in, I warned her about my early morning habits with a twist that put me in a desirable light.

"I get up every morning at the crack of dawn," I told her. "I have to because I'm still a counselor at heart, so each morning, I meet with a group of struggling alcoholics and volunteer my time as a pro-bono counselor in group therapy sessions."

The sparkle in her eyes made it clear that she was proud of me. Philanthropy is a great way to hide shame, and sober meetings came with an element of shame.

As Ava began to bring out the light in my life, the darkness didn't appreciate it. By mid-November, two weeks before meeting her parents for the first time, that darkness started beckoning with a vengeance, sending me into relapse.

The morning before the relapse began the same as usual. We worked together to make breakfast on a hot plate set up in the corner of our cold concrete floor in our makeshift living room. We set our dishes to soak so that when we got home, we could easily scrape the unevenly cooked oatmeal from the steel pot.

She fluffed her hair, somehow making herself look like a runway model, and took off in her tank of a jeep for her classes toward a degree in biology. I slid my feet into my trusty cowboy boots, pulling up my jeans and straightening them back down over the calf-high leather. From the kitchen table, I grabbed my big book from the sober meetings, which was filled with short sayings that helped me stay away from booze. Walking down the street to my meeting, I began putting on the mask I needed to avoid relapse.

After the meeting, I strolled the quiet town for an hour to kill time, before assuming my post at my current job in a musty, dimly lit ski shop. Whitefish has a ghostly feel in the fall. With ski season on its way and dustings of snow occasionally falling, anticipation builds while the excitement has to be squelched for another month. This creates cultural frustration and tension throughout town. Once ski season settles in with its seven-month-long blanket of frosty snow pillows, it becomes hard not to feel as if vacation is a daily reality.

In a reflective state and concentrating on the melancholic atmosphere, I took my post on the stool behind the counter of the shop. Within ten minutes, I was bored out of my skin. Days could go by in the fall without a single customer. That particular day, my mind began getting the best of me. It's far too easy to hear the true emotions between your ears when there are no visitors to steal the silence with gleeful hellos.

Six hours later, customers would come in, but they weren't there to buy ski gear. Instead, they were there for ladies' night, the low-fi entertainment that could help with the desperate fall-time ski town blues. Women from every surrounding city flooded in to take advantage of the free wine and cheese and the special feeling of a night designed for them. Pouring glasses of warm boxed wine for the ladies who stumbled through the threshold of our somber storefront took a toll on my fragile, impressionable mind.

As I caved in on myself, I thought, *I don't deserve the woman who just tattooed a ring to her finger. She doesn't even know me.* She was in her world, believing we had something great together, while I was barely making it around the clock without succumbing to my alcoholic despair and suicidal thinking. The man I showed her didn't exist. He was a character casting dramatic shadows on an empty auditorium.

The solution to my emptiness was within arm's reach, and it was free. So it wasn't much beyond an hour before the wine had turned my teeth purple and was sloshing around inside me. I washed it all down with a few milligrams of Xanax.

Ava and I had created a vacation rental out of my family's cabin while we lived in the basement, and sometime during my shift, guests arrived. Filled to the brim with spirits after having abstained for six months, I was ready and eager to entertain the traveling patrons. I ran home, greeted them with hugs, and amped up the party. To spice things up, I entered the code to my safe, where I had hidden a couple hundred hits of LSD. I bit off five doses for myself and offered our guests a tab. They declined, but I was already spiraling toward the bleak oblivion I cherished so dearly, all alone and the king of none like Ziggy Stardust. When Ava got home my wish was granted. I was kicked out of the house and left to trip the rest of the evening on my own. My head spun around and the night whipped by in a psychedelic blur. I don't remember much, besides finishing the last of my beer hunched over in some bushes near my home, hiding from something my mind had made up.

I also had at least a few beers hidden in the house. In the various recesses that a 1920s-built home offers, I could store anything from half-gallon jugs to cases. I could reach my hand into any dark, spider web-filled cubby and was almost guaranteed to find a solution to my worries, doubts, loneliness, and boredom.

Since the front door was used for our guests, I stepped up to the back door. It was locked, and I didn't have the key.

I needed the beer inside, so my respect for the guests, our neighbors, my wife, and God disappeared quicker than a shadow in sunlight. I picked up a garbage can and hurled it at the door, and the echoing bang ricocheted throughout our small neighborhood.

When the garbage can didn't work, I got in my truck. It was almost 8:00 a.m., and the local beer lockers were about to open. I could get to the gas station, steal a beer, and come back with newfound wit and creativity that would help me find a way inside the house.

I pulled the truck out with the kind of eagerness usually only reserved for a man driving his wife to the hospital to give birth. I flew through stop signs in general disregard for any life, my own included.

With the beer finally in my hand, I sat in my truck, feeling like I'd just scored an A on an exam I didn't study for.

The next thing I knew, police lights ripped through the morning dew on the truck's windshield. I opened the door and was quickly shoved to the concrete with handcuffs pulling my shoulders in unnatural ways and cutting into my wrists. Surely, it was a mistake.

Tight, shaking, and cold inside the jail cell, my body and mind began to come back to reality. One eye poked through the forest of my LSD-clouded mind and peered through the vibrating, waving tendrils of psychedelic fiber. The concrete blocks unified for a split second before spreading out and falling away, as the drug pulled me back under into the mysterious space behind my eyes.

I tried to gain my footing. I heard a long, slow grinding followed by a loud clink of heavy metal. *Oh, I know exactly where I am. Jail.*

Another louder clash was followed by a blinding light

pouring into my cell. As my eyes came into focus, I saw the shadowy figure of a large man outlined by waves of the intense light.

A friendly sounding voice said, "Mark Turnipseed, here's breakfast. Eat it quick. Your transport will be here soon." The voice trailed off, replaced by the brutal sensation of the metal door clanging shut, encasing me again in my cell.

I was alone, and the lights weren't on. The voice bringing my food was kind. *I must be in Whitefish,* I thought. *Thank God. Maybe I can talk my way out of this and get back to that six-pack I just stole from the gas station.*

For a couple of hours, I fought a fake battle between eternal damnation and one more chance on earth with a God I knew nothing about. I believed I was starting to descend into the first layer of hell. So in my horrific LSD nightmare, I was kicking with every ounce of strength I could muster. I needed a chance to present another plea to heaven's great judge.

Then, memory and consciousness began to reluctantly break through before my kick was no longer strong enough to prevent me from sliding into the flames for good.

It was a bad relapse, but the consequences that came later were much worse. A broken door, shattered window, and frightened vacation rental guests were only the tip of the iceberg. The real me was out, and he was furious, hungry, and rabid.

This first relapse after marrying Ava marked a left turn down a road that the two of us would come to call "the trials." During the next couple of months, I relived every demon from my childhood and attempted every solution at the expense of my marriage.

Shattered by a trash can, my insecurities and fears were resting on our doorstep like a big real estate sign. But Ava was a woman who protected her home, mind, dreams, and values with a fury and strength only seen in Greek Mythology. She had married a strong, sober man with a heart of gold, and she was determined to settle for nothing less. Unfortunately, I wasn't the only one in denial.

TWENTY-SIX

THE PLUNGE

These are the thoughts of an addict trying to figure his way out of hell:

Here I am again at a very familiar spot, and I've run out of ideas. I guess it's finally time I start taking the suggestions of this damn sober group.

Or maybe I should just give up, which means I'll most likely die of an overdose or in another serious skiing accident. But I wasn't even able to drink myself to death after that. Lord knows I tried.

Look at that pool. Mom used to think I'd be able to be in the Olympics or at least an elite college swimmer. She said I had the shoulders for it. Wouldn't that have been cool? My life would be made right now if I'd kept swimming.

Okay, well, maybe not. But I probably wouldn't be sitting here wondering what to do with myself. I'd probably at least be healthy. It's too bad I quit at such a young age, and all because I didn't want to wear a speedo. I did like swimming. Maybe I'd like it again. There's that guy in the sober group who does the Ironman Triathlon. Maybe I could do something radical like that. Who knows? Fuck it.

I'm just gonna hop in and see what happens. At least I wouldn't have to wear a speedo like I did on the youth swim team. I might as well come out as gay if I wear a speedo.

God, if I actually work this sober program, will I really have to share that I like men? They say it's important to tell your secrets, and I guess I get why.

Giving up sounds pretty good compared to rattling off my sexual thoughts. But not yet. Let's see what this swimming thing is all about.

Two weeks after a relapse that nearly ended my life and my marriage, I jumped into the pool and swam four lengths. Two laps. I got out huffing, puffing, blue, and dizzy. Sliding over the edge of the pool like a slug in mud, I stumbled toward the sauna like a zombie. A guy next to me babbled about a triathlon he'd done the previous year that wasn't too far from our town.

That guy looked like all he did was eat. I'm glad he's gone. I really hate smelling other people in the sauna, especially when they're gross.

God, I'm such a horrible person. I really do just think the world revolves around me, and I'm so judgmental. They say in the program that's the reason why I drink. The slogan goes, "selfishness and self-centeredness—we think that's the root of all our problems" or something like that. Maybe I should ask that fella who always talks about Ironman Triathlon to explain more about that saying. He's always reciting stuff word-for-word out of the book they follow, like it's some Bible. I hate that big blue book. I love the meetings and the coffee, but that book is just horrible. Old, sexist, preachy type writing about God and prayer.

You know, if that guy could do a triathlon, maybe I could. I'd be pretty proud of myself if I completed one. And there really isn't too much in my life that I'm proud of at this minute.

I've got a long road to repair my marriage and a long road before sobriety will finally settle in. But I just swam pretty good. I mean, I'm tired, but shit, if I gave it a few months, I'll bet I could do one of those Ironman things.

I'll bet if I told Ava I'm going to do a triathlon, she would be proud of me. It might give her something to hope for. I mean, if I'm training, at least she'd know I wasn't drinking. Plus, I'm sure she'd like the triathlon body I'll get.

I'm gonna do it! I'm gonna go home and let Ava know that I've decided to do a triathlon. I should probably add something about sobriety in there, too. She's taking this relapse thing pretty seriously. Maybe she'd trust me with money again and give me my debit card back. Honestly, I don't trust me with money either. Booze is just too accessible, and it's too easy to fall back on.

It's scary to bring up this triathlon thing with all that's going on. A few beers before telling her would sure make it easier. But crap, no money. Well, I still have my Xanax. I know I have a serious problem with it, but I'll never admit that. I should probably take one now. I can let the medicine work on my anxiety so that I can talk about the triathlon when Ava gets home. Somehow, I'll need to get her to pay for it.

I have enough time to clean up the house, and I'll take the dogs out just before she's supposed to get home. She'll be thrilled that I did these chores. She'll be lying in bed, happy, and proud of her hard-working, house-cleaning, dog-walking husband. Then, I'll tell her about the triathlon. I hate walking these dogs.

"Ava?" I said while opening the front door. Our three big dogs tore through the open door like soldiers invading a castle. *Why do they do that?* I asked myself. *I really don't like dogs anymore. They kind of piss me off.*

"Ava? Are you home?" I said a little louder.

"Down here, reading," she said with a somber tone.

Great. She doesn't sound thrilled about the dog-walking or the house-cleaning. She doesn't really sound like she's in a good mood at all. I guess I can't blame her. I mean, I did just get out of jail. But she took me back and moved back in. I didn't ruin absolutely everything. And I'm going to do a triathlon!

"Hey babe, I've got something to tell you," I said with a slight shake in my voice. "You know that guy I talk about from the sober group? Jim?"

"Yeah, isn't he the guy you hate?"

"Yeah, but he does an Ironman Triathlon, and he's been sober for like thirty years. I was thinking that maybe if I did one I'd be able to stay sober, too."

Silence.

"What do you think?" I continued.

"Well, I think you're crazy," she said with her head still buried in her book. "I don't see why you can't just do something like a half-marathon or something. Do you think you'll ever be able to do something, good or negative, without going to the extreme?"

Hold back, Mark—that was clearly a rhetorical question, I told myself.

"I mean, Jesus, Mark," she said, now looking up from her book. Her eyes were stern, but oh, so beautiful. Every time I looked into them, I felt like a little boy again. "Two weeks ago, you went to jail for domestic disturbance while drunk and on acid, and now, you want to do an Ironman?"

Crap. My heart was sinking, but I wanted to argue my point. A triathlon could be healthy for my sobriety. Why couldn't she see this? I decided I had better hold back, though, since I was in the "dog house."

She looked up at the ceiling as if caught in a dream, clearly sorting through her thoughts. "That's the way you work—extremes. I've kind of accepted it."

Then, her tone changed. "I think it would be a great thing for you to do," she said.

"Really!?"

I had already decided which race I wanted to do, and I had the website open on my laptop on the floor beside our bed. We slept in a tiny, partially finished basement room with no furniture besides a mattress. We didn't even have a closet, so we hung our clothes on the exposed pipes over our heads. It was like a dungeon with egress windows no larger than a TV screen on the back of an airplane seat.

And here she was, encouraging me to follow my crazy dream while living in a dungeon. I really had gotten lucky.

Since we had very little money, I was scared to tell her what was involved. She had just purchased a gym membership for me, and I was sure that after she saw the Ironman registration fee, she would flip.

"Uhhhh…can I use your card to pay the entrance fee?"

No response. Without saying anything, she reached over her body and twisted slightly while shuffling through something on the floor. She came back up with her debit card and flung it over to me.

I shut my mouth and began typing in the information before she changed her mind.

"Okay, I'm in! We're going to North Carolina in October!"

"How does it feel?" she said with very little emotion.

"Scared. It's scary as shit. I can't believe I just did that."

"There's no turning back now, Mark."

I nodded, realizing she was right.

"Oh, and you should probably find another one for practice—one earlier in the season."

Going along with her suggestion, I signed up for an Olympic distance triathlon just five months away. Then, I had the Ironman 70.3 in eight months. I was locked in.

By the end of the year, I would be able to call myself a triathlete. This was going to be a piece of cake. All I had to do was learn how to swim better. I already knew how to run and bike.

But later that night, my emotions shifted. I tossed and turned, unable to sleep. I was in a panic. The commitment I had made was absurdly beyond anything I'd ever done, and since Ava was financially invested, I had to give it my best. I couldn't back out.

This damn downloaded triathlon training plan is ridiculous, I told myself. It was a PDF called "Beginner Olympic triathlon 3-month plan." The workouts were outrageous. Who on earth could bike that much and then run on a treadmill right after for multiple days in a row? I was used to working out for an hour, then taking two to three days off before I headed back to the gym. Most days on this program required two workouts in a single day!

This is going to suck. I can't believe I got myself into it.

When I arrived at the gym, fear settled in. I knew my way around the weight room fairly well, but in my years of intermittent gym exploits, I had avoided the cardio machines. The plan said it was supposed to be a "conversational seven-mile run," but since I didn't know what that meant, I decided I would run seven miles as hard as I could go.

That can't be too hard, right? I hope none of my friends sees me sweating and cursing.

Ten minutes in, and I was cruising!

Man, I feel invincible. I can see myself getting used to this. It isn't hard at all. I was breathing like a banshee, but my mind pushed me through the cardiovascular stress. I could see why people ran for stress reduction.

I wonder if I have the right form, I asked myself. *I wonder if I look attractive up here, or if I look like one of those people that I hate to even walk by while they're huffing and puffing on the treadmill. I sure hope I look good. I feel good. Shit, I know this guy coming up the stairs. I hope he doesn't choose the treadmill beside me.*

Luckily, he put his stuff on a treadmill three down from me.

Good. There's no way I can have a conversation. Shit, he's coming over.

"Mark!" I nodded my head in response, but I almost lost my footing in the process. He saw the struggle and said, "Oh, sorry, man. I don't want to disturb you. Have a good run!"

All I could say through gasping was, "You, too!"

When I looked down at the treadmill, I saw that I'd made it six miles. One mile left.

I'm a rock star. No, wait—I'm a triathlete!

My ego boomed, and I took off down the last mile by cranking the speed up a little bit. I was running a seven-minute mile. I figured that must be a good pace because my life insurance said I could get discounts if I could run a seven-minute mile.

I'll show 'em.

Upon completion, I stretched all sexy-like, checking behind

me to see if anyone was looking. My butt and legs already felt like they could be in an underwear commercial.

Damn, this feels good. But no one's looking, so screw stretching. A steam would be good.

It was hot and cloudy in the steam room. Perfect. The sauna was too personal. In the steam room, you could make out bodies but not faces. Plus, the sauna allowed women, while the steam room was only men, mostly nude. I got settled, and the door opened.

"Mark, is that you?" the voice said.

"Yeah. Is that you, Sterling?"

"Yeah, dude. Hey, I didn't know you were a runner."

He came in and bared his naked body. He was in great shape.

My heart began to race, and I hoped that he would sit close enough for me to keep checking him out. I had gotten lucky in the steam room once. Maybe this could be number two.

Sterling sat down about ten feet away.

Crap. Well, if I cheat on my wife, I'll feel like shit. Wouldn't that just be the cherry on top of the relapse?

"Yeah, man. I'm doing triathlons now. I'm a triathlete," I said with pride.

"Oh, sweet! Well, more power to ya. I don't know how you guys do all three. My wife and I have run a few marathons and just got done with an ultramarathon."

"Yeah, triathlon is a rough life, but it's not too bad," I said, completely disinterested in his experience while eager to boast and brag about my false life as a triathlete.

It's my first day of training. Why do I already consider myself a triathlete? God, I've got some problems. But I already said it, so now, I have to stick with it. I can't wait to find Jim in the morning and tell him my plan to do an Ironman. He's going to be impressed.

"Well, Sterling, I've got to go." Clearly, he wasn't going to let me get him off, so I thought I might as well leave.

"I'll be seeing you on the treadmill. Good luck with your training," he said as I walked out without my towel around me, hoping he made one last suggestion while looking at my newly sculpted butt and tight runner's legs.

But he didn't. I still felt pretty successful for running seven miles like it was nothing. I was a bad ass. A triathlete.

TWENTY-SEVEN

WHAT THE SHIT?

The next morning, my alarm clock awakened me at 6:00 a.m. Usually, I would get up to pee sometime during the night, but I had just slept through everything.

I flung my legs over the bedside, and lightning pain shot through my leg muscles. I tried to stand up but could barely move. I had to roll over, put my hands on the side of the bed, and gently push myself up with my legs straight. I wasn't going to try to bend those suckers again.

I managed to stand up but walked to the bathroom, feeling like an amputee pirate with pegs for legs. *My God, maybe I'm not quite the athlete I thought I was. How the fuck am I supposed to swim and bike today?*

I was actually excited to go to my sober group meeting that morning. I could show off to Jim and explain why I was so sore. He'd surely think more of me.

But then, I thought, *Why am I even concerned about what Jim thinks about me? I don't even like him. But damn, that man is so intense and so confident. I do wish I had some of that.*

Ava was absolutely adamant that I go to every meeting I could. Since I didn't have a job anymore, there was no reason why I couldn't make it to all of them. So where did my thoughts go?

I'd better find a job soon. Maybe I'll be an Uber driver. That sounds fun. If I end up fucking things up and losing my wife, I'll at least have enough money to get drunk.

God, I'm sick. My thoughts are like 10,000 leagues from where they're supposed to be. I'd better go to a meeting. It's getting late.

The meeting started at 7:00 a.m., but what would normally take me five minutes to walk took me twenty minutes on my pirate legs.

Once I got there, I couldn't wait for the meeting to be over. Jim was there, wearing all of his Ironman garb.

That guy talks about how a big ego causes us to drink, but he sure doesn't seem to do anything about his. What a show-off.

"Hello, Mark. Why are you walking so funny today?" Jim asked when he saw me.

Ha! He noticed! I don't have to come up with some roundabout way of introducing him to his new Ironman colleague.

"I started training for an Ironman," I said with pride.

"That wasn't my question. I asked why you're walking that way."

God, this guy is just so unpleasant. I swear there's no way to buy acceptance from this man. He makes me feel bad about myself every time I talk to him. How could he not be proud?!

"That's why I'm walking like this because I'm so sore from my run," I said with a whine in my voice.

Why do I care so much what he thinks about me?

"Well, I've been doing Ironman for fifteen years, and I've

never walked like that. You must be doing something wrong. Do you have a coach?"

"Well, I ran so hard that…well, no, I don't have a coach, but I do have a plan that I downloaded from the internet."

Why don't I just walk away? He obviously isn't about to give me any praise or sympathy. This sucks.

"A plan is good, but a coach is better. How about recovery? How is repairing things with Ava going? Sounds like your last relapse was intense."

Suddenly, I was in one of those conversations that's worse than cleaning toilets with a toothbrush.

"Well, it's okay. We haven't talked about it too much. I'm just going to keep coming to meetings and make sure I don't drink."

"Do you have a sponsor?"

This is sounding strangely similar to our Ironman discussion.

"Well, no, but I have a plan, man," I said stubbornly.

I wish he'd just get off my back. I guess I asked for it by waiting around for him. Why the hell did I do that? I was just looking for some validation and acceptance, and I got the complete opposite. Now, I feel bad about myself, my triathlon idea, and my sobriety. Screw this guy.

"Well, hey, Mark, if you want a coach for the triathlon, I would be more than happy to help."

"Okay, Jim, I'll think about it."

No, I won't. I don't want him as a coach. How could he coach me when all he does is make me feel bad about myself?

"Have a good day," I said, as I went home feeling downcast and frustrated.

Ava had breakfast on the table and was sipping a warm cup of coffee when I arrived. The steam was rising through the air and dissipating as it came into contact with the beautiful rays of sun shining through the kitchen window.

"You're so kind, Ava. I love you."

"I love you, too, Mark, but honestly, it's not easy to make breakfast for you right now. I'm still horribly upset."

Why would she express something like that right now? Doesn't she know it's just going to piss me off? Everyone is pissing me off today.

"Yeah, well, I won't mess up again." Of course, I wasn't going to let her know that her words angered me. I didn't share those feelings with others because I knew they would just hold the information against me.

"I ran into Jim today," I continued, "and he wants to be my triathlon coach."

Ava laughed.

I kept talking. "I think he also wants to be my sponsor, but he's just offering because he feels bad for me. He's probably at his house, telling his wife about me and laughing right now."

"Mark, don't you realize that some people actually care about you? Like me. I actually love you. But you think all these people are out to get you and make fun of you. He would be an excellent sponsor. Didn't you say your past sponsors were too soft on you? Maybe he's just what you need."

I shouldn't let people know about things like how my past sponsors were too soft. See how she uses my private life against me? But maybe, just maybe she's trying to help. Maybe Jim really is trying to help.

Fuck it. I'm going to the gym for my workout. Today is swim and bike. I can do this. I don't care what Jim says. I'm already a triathlete.

I was sore, but I was able to finish my swimming and biking workouts. When I got home, I was glad to find that Ava was already gone for work. I ordered a pizza and picked out a scary movie on Netflix. This was going to be a perfect night!

I'm so impressed with myself and my workouts today. What does Jim know anyway? I'm sure showing him. And sobriety? Look at me, ordering pizza, staying in, and not even thinking about booze.

But when I stood up to answer the door, I felt a sudden pop in my left Achilles heel, causing me to fall to my knees and clutch my ankle. I managed to pull myself up and hobble to the front door to get my pizza.

The pain was intense, so I began to worry that I had ripped my Achilles tendon. I texted the only person I knew to ask about it: Jim.

"Have you ever felt a horrible pop on the back of your heel after hard training?" I typed into my phone.

"No," he texted back. "Did that happen to you? You really need a coach before you hurt yourself."

My thinking got ugly again. *This guy is probably sitting over at his house laughing about how pathetic I am. I need a drink. Luckily, I have some money stashed away.*

When Ava got home, I was asleep. "It smells like beer in here," she said. "Have you been drinking?"

"No way!" I answered, as I rolled over. "I'm asleep."

I heard her moving things around like she was looking for empty bottles. I could hear her breathing heavily as she started to move heavier stuff in her search.

"Can you stop that?" I yelled. "What the hell are you doing?"

I jumped out of bed. "What the fuck, Ava?"

I pushed her, and then, I blacked out, which always happened faster when I was angry.

If I knew the remaining details of this story, I would share it. Upon awakening, however, Ava was gone, and there was a lot of broken glass. When I looked at my phone, I saw one text from her. It was a video file of me smashing a huge mirror and running toward her with a broken shard in my hand as though I were trying to kill her. Then, I fell to the ground and made horrible noises.

Watching that video caused me to lose all faith in myself. I felt terrified of the monster I had become. It wrecked my soul.

But that was exactly why I needed a drink.

It was only 6:00 a.m., but I found the hidden bottle of liquor that I had stashed the night before. I couldn't remember drinking any of it, but there were only a couple of sips left.

The stores didn't open the beer vaults until 8:00 a.m.

I couldn't get over what I had done to Ava, but I was also instantly reminded that it wasn't the first time. I had been that angry and confused plenty of times.

I'd never felt as scared as I did while watching that video, though. I could have killed her.

I didn't expect Ava to come back home, but she did.

"Mark? We need to talk."

I rolled off the couch and got my footing. My legs were still sore from the training, and my heel was killing me. The empty pizza box on the coffee table was beginning to smell. It made me want to vomit.

"I'm leaving if you don't get help. And if you drink again, I won't come back," she continued. "You need to take Jim up on his offer to help you. Allow him to sponsor you through the twelve steps. If you don't, I'm really going to leave."

All I could think was: *I can't handle this. Jim doesn't know what he's talking about. Ava doesn't know what she's talking about. I know what I'm doing. Maybe I should go to the hot springs where I'll soak to make my body feel better and set up a sex date with that girl I met. That'll make the hole in my heart feel better. I need someone who doesn't care about the things going on in my life right now, because frankly, I don't care either.*

And with that, I grabbed my swimsuit and ran past my crying wife.

"Mark?" she said, choking back her tears. "Please, let's get this figured out. I'm scared!"

I was scared, too, but I couldn't show it. My solution was always to forget about my fears with substances and sex.

When I got out of the hot springs, I was lost in the excitement of hooking up with the girl who just wanted me to use her while she used me. But then, I got a text message from her: "What about your wife? She told me you're hurting her badly by talking to me."

What the fuck? Okay, maybe I don't need anyone in my life. I hope Ava isn't there when I get back. I made a big mistake marrying her. I don't even like women. They just make me feel sexy and good about myself. What the fuck am I doing?

I looked down at my phone and switched to the Grindr app. There was a message that intrigued me. A guy had sent a picture of himself, and he was gorgeous.

I started my car, but the blue sky and fresh ranch air became annoyances as the drive turned into labor. I couldn't sit still, and none of my music took the edge off.

So I pulled into the next gas station and grabbed a forty-ounce bottle of beer.

I was afraid Ava would be at home, so I didn't want to go back. If only I had a sleeping bag.

When I walked in the door of the house, I heard calming music coming from our bedroom.

What is this? Makeup sex? I hate makeup sex. When I'm angry, I just think about how much I wish I wasn't with a woman.

When I opened the bedroom door, I saw Ava lying on the bed but fully dressed.

"Mark," she said calmly, "I can't believe what I heard today. You don't believe in our marriage. You don't believe in me. And you want *her!?*" She held up her phone like she was directing traffic and showed me a picture of the girl I had texted.

I felt ashamed.

"You took this picture in OUR bedroom?!" This time, she showed me a photo of my own naked body.

I stood there speechless, but inside, I was raging with anger.

"I'm done. I'm never coming back!" Ava said as she walked out of the bedroom.

I was furious with the girl for sending my text messages to my wife. I picked up my phone and sent a series of horrible messages to her, but they did nothing to ease my anger.

I knew what would. I had beer in my truck, and there was a guy on Grindr who wanted to have sex with me.

I spent the next hour getting drunk. I also called my psychiatrist, apologized for not seeing him for a few months, and asked if he would write me another prescription for my anxiety pills. He did.

For the next couple of days, I stayed in the basement while

our vacation rental guests were upstairs. As usual, I nursed my emotional wounds in my cave with beer and pills.

I began to chastise myself for treating Ava so badly. *Why do I treat everyone I love this way? All they want to do is care for me and help me, and I hurt them because they do. I don't even get to see my precious baby boy because of it. He probably doesn't even know me anymore. I'm such a failure in every way. I barely made it through college, and I can't stay sober to save my life. The world would be better without me.*

Where are my pills?

I had a month supply of Xanax, but before I took them, I needed to let everyone know.

I'll take a picture of them in my hand and then one in my mouth with a message that says "goodbye," I told myself.

After I sent the messages and took the pills, I knew it wouldn't take long to slip into unconsciousness. As my vision faded to black, my heart would slow to a slight flutter. Then, I'd glide for the rest of time into oblivion. Free at last.

BEEEP, BEEEP, BEEEP!

What the fuck? My eyes opened slightly, and I saw clean, baby blue medical instruments and privacy curtains. I turned my head to the side. It hurt so much that it felt like a train had smashed my brain.

Then, I saw Ava sitting beside my hospital bed.

I closed my eyes again. *I hope she didn't see me wake up.*

I wasn't ready to talk to her. I never wanted to talk to her or face her again. I never wanted to face anything in my life again. I wanted to die.

"Mark?" she said.

Since I didn't have any self-control while that inebriated, I responded in spite of myself. "Yes?"

"Why did you want to die?"

"Because I've fucked up too much. There's no coming back."

"You fucked up, but there's a good person in you. I married a good person. Don't you think you have plenty to live for?"

"Not right now."

"Well, you have another chance."

"Are you going to come back home, Ava?"

"Yes, Mark. I'm here for you. I believe in you. I believe in us."

TWENTY-EIGHT

GOODBYE #2

Two weeks after I got out of the hospital, Ava was still around, but our marriage was also still on the brink of collapse.

At least my time in the sober meetings was going well. I talked with Jim a lot, and we had a deep discussion about acceptance. I began to see his points more clearly. I also had begun to feel respect and a love and deep gratitude for him.

My injury also subsided, and I started to make progress with my triathlon training. That's likely because I stopped acting as though I was a professional triathlete and accepted that I had a long way to go. I accepted myself through the difficulties of training.

I also realized that accepting myself meant I had to start letting other people in. I couldn't remain an island in the process. I had to be willing to ask for help and acceptance from others.

I decided that I would come clean to Ava the next day about who I truly was. She needed to know about my childhood confusion and my sexuality.

I made an elaborate brunch for her so that we could talk when she came home after her 9:00 a.m. class. It was a colorful dish of sweet potato hash with kale, Brussels sprouts, and tomatoes over eggs.

I was so nervous. Once I told her, there would be no coming back. Maybe I could blame it on my relative who molested me. I could say I used to be bisexual, and I didn't like men anymore. I could say I had become straight as an arrow.

By the time Ava got home, I truly believed the lies I had been telling myself in my head. *Since it was all from the childhood trauma, we can move on,* I thought. *I've healed from my gayness.*

"I have a lot to tell you today, Ava," I said as I motioned her toward the table.

"I know. I'm sure you do," she said as she sat across from me.

"So ... for the majority of my life," I began, "I have been pretty confused and filled with a lot of shame about it. I'm beginning to see that all this stuff I'm about to tell you is what makes me feel the need to drink. I guess that's why we share it with someone else. It takes the power out of the past and places the power into our own hands. Supposedly, after acknowledging and accepting it, I regain power in my life. And I need that Ava. I'm so sick of feeling weak, ruled by depression and substances. I need to feel free, so I need to tell you everything."

And I did proceed to tell her just about *everything* . . . from the childhood beauty fort contest to the youth rehab programs to my sexual deviance while hooked on heroin. Her face dropped, but at the same time, her eyes brightened.

"Thank you so much for sharing all that with me," she said finally. "You've been through a lot."

I had thought she would make fun of me when she heard about the bisexual stuff, but she didn't even flinch. I wondered what she would have said if I had told her the full truth—that I still liked men and always did, even before the beauty fort incident with my relative. But what I did tell her was all I could handle.

"Thanks for letting me share all of that with you," I told her. "I know some of it might have been hard to hear. Just know that I'm healed now, and things are going to get better."

"Mark, I don't know how to tell you this, but I won't believe it until I start to see it," Ava said gently.

That wasn't the way it was supposed to go! She was supposed to accept me, and I was supposed to get my power back, I thought.

Jim said things would get better, but I saw no evidence of success yet. How was I to believe anything would improve?

I stormed out of the house and headed to the gym to swim. My first race would be 1650 yards, but so far, I could barely swim 500 yards without stopping. I would have to run more than thirteen miles. I could barely run six or seven at that point. I began to think of myself as weak.

The anger I felt about Ava's response clouded my progress and replaced my confidence with fear. *I'm going to fail at everything,* I thought.

As soon as that thought hit, I gave up again. I knew the perfect bridge to jump from. I wasn't going to warn anyone this time, so I wouldn't fail. But I wanted my dog Buddy with me. He'd been my loyal companion since freshman year of college. A tall, black lab with long legs, his paws were as big as a lion's. He towered above other labs his age. He had watched me as I shot up heroin and looked at me with grave disappointment on those occasions when I couldn't get up from the couch.

After filling my truck with vodka and beer, I loaded Buddy into the back and hopped in the driver's seat. When I got to the bridge, the sun was still out, so I had to keep driving and drinking until it was dark. I listened to only my favorite music. After all, they would be my last tunes.

A few hours later, I was drunk enough. I had driven miles away from town, finding myself on top of Desert Mountain. The bridge was at the base of this mountain, and it was perched over the river where I once worked as a raft guide. I was saying goodbye in my own way this time.

I had always felt this place was magical. I peered over the seemingly endless landscape and suddenly felt a sense of life. The sun was setting, causing the bright colors of day to splash against the horizon and fade into cool pastels. It sent rays of hope my way.

Maybe this life is worth it, I thought. *If I subtract all the troubles and pain and just concentrate on the beauty, life is surely worthwhile.*

But then, I looked down at my phone and thought about all the ways I had disappointed and hurt people. I thought about how hard and long the road to redemption would be.

I started to think about Jim. *If it weren't for him, I wouldn't be here.*

No, wait! It's my fault I'm here. I can't turn it around now.

The road down the mountain to the bridge I'd jump from was long and winding with switchbacks that turned sharp, nearing ninety degrees. But I was so drunk that I didn't even notice them. I barreled down the road like nothing mattered. And it didn't. If I flew off the side of the mountain, that would take care of everything.

But wait, I have my dog back there. My precious dog! He has seen me go through so much.

I turned to look back, but where was Buddy?

Buddy? Oh no! Did I leave him?

I stopped my car and called his name a few times.

Oh, well, it's probably best that he doesn't watch the upcoming events.

The bridge wasn't tall enough to kill me on impact, but the river beneath was cold enough. Ice chunks were still floating downriver. Buddy would probably have jumped in after me. I'd have hated to take him with me.

Once I got to the bridge, I was so drunk that I'd almost forgotten what I was doing. I finished the rest of the vodka and beers until I blacked out. Oblivion—the place I loved most.

The next thing I knew, my phone startled me. I had missed thirty calls and too many texts to read. Calls from Ava, my sister, my best friend John, and others. John's message said I deserved to live and that so many people loved me.

Tears began to stream down my face. Strangely enough, I didn't feel like a failure for not managing to end my life the night before.

People do care. I could finally see that. Ava's message said she had been driving around with John, trying to find me. "Please don't die," she said.

How could she still be there for me when I couldn't be there for myself? Why did all of these people care so much for me after all I'd done? And why couldn't I just let them love me?

Acceptance. I needed to accept myself maybe. Accept who I was and the work that needed to be done. I needed to keep training and accept that I wasn't a triathlete yet. I needed to keep going to meetings. I needed to keep sharing and letting others in. I still wasn't an open book—not yet. I needed to believe. Could I?

It's too late for me to believe in myself, I thought. I have no faith in myself.

But maybe, just maybe, I could believe in something else. Maybe I could believe in my training program and start making my way toward triathlete status. Maybe I could start believing that the sober group could work for me like it did for others. Maybe I could slowly learn more about myself besides the fact that I was an alcoholic and a drug addict.

Acceptance and belief. I think I can do that. Maybe one day, I'll begin to believe in myself. Maybe one day, I can end up giving back and begin helping other people. Maybe I can use my story.

By the time I got home, the sun had just begun to rise. Ava was exhausted but also relieved that I was alive.

Still, there was no sign of Buddy. Where was he?

We called around until we finally found out he was at a pound in the next city. He had taken a big fall, which meant I had to face that he must have been thrown out of the back of my truck while I was flying down the Desert Mountain road.

On the drive to pick him up, I couldn't believe I had even hurt my dog. I had hurt everyone.

It's time for that to stop, I told myself firmly. *I'm done with not believing in who I am. I hurt my dog. I'm capable of inflicting much more pain if I keep drinking, but everyone around me says I'm a person of great potential. They keep believing in me, so it's damn time I try to believe it, too.*

Did I have the tools, both physically and mentally, to endure the demands of both sobriety and the triathlon? Would I relapse again under pressure? I didn't know.

TWENTY-NINE

CHILDREN

"Maybe we should have a baby," Ava blurted out.

Two weeks before my first try at a triathlon, she had contacted my ex-wife Callie to arrange for a visit with my son River. I hadn't seen him in three years—not since I had put him in harm's way. Callie's trust in me was thinner than a thread of silk, so Ava ensured her that we would honor any of her requests.

Luckily, the visit went well. We played in the lake. I taught him how to whittle with a pocket knife, and we made s'mores by a campfire. Then, on the last day of the visit, Ava and I were allowed to drop River off at school, and it opened the floodgates of my heart.

Upon leaving the school, tears pooled in my eyes, and I had to pull off to the side of the road to cry. I wept for the times I had put him into harms way, and the joy of knowing that if I stayed sober I wouldn't harm him again. But when Ava saw my emotion, her suggestion about our own baby came pouring out.

I was shocked that she would suggest such a thing so soon after I'd put her through hell. It's true that I had been talking non-stop about my sobriety and the triathlon. Either a lesson I learned in sobriety was helping me with the triathlon, or something about the triathlon training was helping me with sobriety.

For one thing, I did get a coach and didn't question his plans for me. Rather than scrutinize the workouts, I discovered that they were much more productive if I just dove right in and did them without question.

The same proved true of sobriety. The more I surrendered to it, the better it went.

I was also surprised that when Ava mentioned she wanted to have a baby, I didn't feel afraid.

When we got home, Ava felt sick. I figured it was car sickness. It wasn't. She was already pregnant.

THIRTY

THE FIRST RACE

Five minutes before the race began, a voice over the loud speaker (very loud) recited all of the instructions that I had already memorized from the pre-race emails. So I decided to use the time to pump myself up.

I'm so thrilled with myself. I believe I can make the distance and probably even win.

I looked around me at the 100 or so other competitors. *I'm clearly stronger and in better shape than 80% of them,* I thought.

The blabbering noise from the race director was finally done. *That took forever. I didn't need to hear any of that. Just let me go. Open the gates!*

10-9-8-7...

My heart was pounding.

... 6-5-4-3-2-BANG!

As soon as the starting gun went off, I jumped into the water like a Navy seal. No one there was going to swim as fast as me!

But less than one minute into the swim, I began to struggle to find my course. Still, I saw no one in front of me.

I'm in first place! See—all you have to do is believe in yourself, Mark!

I made a handful of more powerful strokes before checking on the other swimmers again. The power behind my shoulder was weak, and the lunge forward that was supposed to help me lift my head just wasn't working. It was my first time in structured/competitive swimming, so the directional stroke was important to get right. If I didn't, I would steer off course and waste time going in the wrong direction.

Unfortunately, my arms had already become weak, and so had my sighting stroke. I tried for it again. Putting all of my might into my stroke, I was able to bring my head up and faintly see a buoy in the distance bobbing up and down in the water. I was supposed to swim toward it, and at that point, there was only one swimmer in front of me.

Since my head wasn't fully free of the cold waters during the sighting of the buoy, I took in a huge amount of water into my throat and began coughing.

I'm losing it.

I tried to keep swimming, but my heart began to rev like an engine in the Daytona 500. I panicked and couldn't breathe. It felt like my chest was caving in on itself, and my wetsuit had become alive, strangling me. My throat closed up. I thought my eyes might pop out of their sockets and explode into my goggles.

I tossed my arm up in the air as I rolled on my back. This was the signal for emergencies so that they would send someone in a kayak to pull me out of the water.

As I rolled onto my back and continued to call for help, however, I was reminded of something. Not too long ago, I wasn't able to go into a grocery store if I wasn't drunk. I was barely able to get out of bed or leave my house without the help of copious amounts of weed and pills. My anxiety was so crippling that I hid in my house most days. Some mornings, I was too scared to leave my bed and even go into the living room. I was afraid of seeing the remains of the night before. And I had faced death.

So I had felt this kind of fear before—the kind that spoke total calamity and worst case scenarios.

Mark, it's okay, I told myself. *Slow down now. Remember who you are. Are you here to win this race? Sit back, dude. Look up at the sky while you paddle on your back. Laugh at yourself. Enjoy this time. Just swim the entire mile in back stroke if you have to.*

Occasionally, I rolled over and gave freestyle a try, but inevitably, I wound up out of air after a few strokes. So I had to flip back onto my back, look at the sky, smile, and continue to mosey in back stroke. *This is who I am,* I thought. *I still have a long way to go and a lot to learn about myself and running a triathlon.*

It took me forever to get through the swim part. I was the last one left in the water and beginning to feel ill. It was a good thing that biking, my strong suit, was next. I was going to power through the 25-mile bike ride and catch up to everyone I lost in the water.

When I climbed out and saw the crowd, I again fell into my crutch-mindset that I was "the best." I justified it by telling myself that the swim lapses were just a fluke. I ran by Ava, who cheered for me as if I was in first place. She had a way of complimenting my already inflated ego.

Once on the bike, I pushed as hard as I could. The course was an out-and-back, repeat-style loop. So while you're on the first loop and moving slowly, you can see the people who are in first place as they move quickly past you on their second loop. I was able to pass by a few people within five miles. But as I cruised toward the turnaround halfway point, people started to pass me.

The carbon tires and aerodynamic frames of the elite competitors' bikes made a low rumble, a sound much like a high-speed train entering a tunnel. It filled my stomach with disappointment. The athletes on those bikes cruised past me in perfect form and with seemingly effortless might and power. They were moving at nearly twice my speed.

I'm worthless, I told myself. *I'm such a disappointment.*

I was absolutely beat both mentally and physically, but I completed the twenty-five miles and changed into my running shoes.

Thank God this hell is almost over. I can't believe how badly I'm doing. And there's Ava with a huge smile and outstretched arms.

For more than an hour, she waited for me to finish biking. She brought her hands together and placed them like a funnel to her mouth as she screamed my praises.

She's acting like I'm succeeding. Why is she doing that? I'm doing horribly.

It had started sleeting during the bike ride, and at below forty degrees, the weather was far too cold for a race. But the pain didn't cause me to quit. Instead, I let it reinvigorate me.

My legs went numb as the sound of Ava's cheers became more distant, but her message was still loud and clear.

Remember who you are. Remember that you have a son who looks up to you, and you have another child on the way.

As those thoughts replaced the ones that told me how poorly I was performing, I began to feel like a winner—even as I was losing. Men who were twice my age passed me on the six-mile run. As they neared me, their footsteps sounded like rapid gun-fire compared to my slow hustle. But I realized it didn't matter because I was becoming a champion.

I'm a father, I'm a triathlete, I'm a son, I'm a brother, and I'm a man who's learning what it means to have integrity. I'm a man who's finally learning to be proud of who he is no matter how far back in the pack he slips.

I finished the race in 96th place out of 100. I can't believe I looked around and judged the other athletes. Who was I to think I was better than everyone else? My first triathlon had officially humbled me.

It taught me that believing in myself isn't always enough. Belief gets us to the starting line, while preparation helps us break the ribbon at the finish line. I realized I couldn't be a good father by just believing either. I needed to accept that I'm a work in progress. I had to be willing to put in the hard work, and I had to listen to the people who cared for me and loved me. I had to accept their encouragement.

When Ava and I first met, I told her about a rock I had rolled over with a lawn mower. As I was going to toss it, I noticed a word painted on it: *Integrity.* I told Ava that if I could think of one character trait that personified my father, it would be that one. I told her that when I found that rock, I decided to make a commitment to live with integrity.

I hadn't kept that commitment, and I didn't fully know what the word meant yet. But with time, as I grew to know myself better, I was determined to begin expressing it in my life.

My last three relapses, my suicide attempts, and my first triathlon had come in close succession. All of those experiences helped me recognize three points that were imperative for me to understand before I could stop myself from getting caught in the same traps:

I needed to accept who I was and where I was. Regardless of what happened in my life, I had to accept it. This would be put to the test when the town where I was to do the Ironman was devastated by a hurricane, delaying my race for an entire year. So it became vital to accept myself and live with the person I was becoming.

1. I needed to let others in. I didn't have to do it all on my own. Thank God, because without all of the love and support I received, there's no way I could do it.

2. I needed to believe in the process. I had to trust that accepting who I was and letting others in was going to work out. I needed to stop holding back and believe in the truth around me. The truth, as they always say, will set you free.

THIRTY-ONE

THE IRONMAN BOULDER 70.3

Suddenly, it was less than a month before I would cross my first Ironman 70.3 finish line. I had spent nearly two years sober, as I ate, drank, and slept for this race. The process had taught me so much. I could taste the glory.

As the time drew nearer, I began to wonder: *Would I be as confident about my sobriety if it wasn't for triathlon?*

Physically, there was a time when I couldn't even touch my toes. From a sobriety standpoint, there was a time when I couldn't walk into a grocery store. So the answer to that question was "no." Training for the triathlon had taught me invaluable lessons. It had helped me trust others and gave me faith in the process of life. I no longer feared the man I was becoming because I could feel my emotions and share them. I could ask for support.

I even managed to develop a strong sense of peace. There would always be a lot of work to do, both in sobriety and training, but I felt more confident that I could take on whatever came next.

I wore my first speedo, too, and actually liked it. I loved it so much that I ordered new underwear. I was sure Ava wouldn't like them, but how long had my behavior been all about appearing to be someone else—someone I didn't even like anymore? It made me sick to think about it.

And yes, Ava did freak out when she found out I would wear speedos and when she saw the new underwear I was so proud of. I added to the commotion by telling her I was going to shave my legs like most triathletes.

"It's simply the last thing I have to do to fully embody a triathlete," I told her.

"Well, if you have to shave your legs, you'd better wear long pants and know that I won't be touching those legs. Haven't you already changed enough because of triathlon? I barely know my own husband now. You wear speedos, briefs, short-shorts, and now you're going to shave your legs?!"

In that moment, I sulked back. For the next few days, all I could do was fear the moment I would have to decide whether to shave or not. Would shaving my legs really lead to my wife's rejection? Would I be able to risk losing her touch and acceptance, even if it was something I needed to do for myself? In the past, I wouldn't have even considered risking that rejection because I needed a woman's touch to validate me.

But I had come so far, and shaving my legs felt like the icing on the cake. It was another step toward breaking out of the old shameful Mark into the new sober triathlete.

The night before the Ironman, I had a very early dinner at 3:00 with Ava, my sons River and Elliott, and my father. I had to get to sleep by 7:00 p.m. because the pre-race events would start at 4:00 a.m. I'd been told the pre-race was like a circus, and I didn't want to get lost in it. So I wanted to get up by 2:30 to take a light jog, awaken my core with some planks and crunches, eat a small carbohydrate-rich breakfast, and set up my gear. That gear took up a whole section of my suite in the hotel.

Before bed, I hopped into the shower with a new razor and some shaving cream. *Here goes nothing,* I thought. I lathered up one entire leg and started at my ankle. It was a stretch to remain balanced while I carefully, yet anxiously, yielded the blade across my skin. I dragged it up my leg until it reached mid-calf. When I looked at my progress, I saw that the razor had only taken about a half-inch of hair even though I had covered nearly seven inches of my leg. The blade was already fully clogged.

This is going to take a very, very long time.

I took a deep breath and reminded myself that everything about a triathlon takes a very, very long time. The thought made me laugh. If I were to introduce the man I was three years ago to the man I had become, the old me would have pointed and jeered. The new me, however, could stomp that sad boy down just by standing next to him.

An hour and a half later, my legs were silky smooth. It felt amazing as I glided moisturizer over my skin. I loved the feeling. Why on earth was I so scared of it? I checked myself out in the mirror and noticed the muscles on my calf protruding through my skin—muscles that had been hidden by the blanket of hair. I could feel the wall AC unit blowing from across the hotel room. Its coolness felt alien.

It's going to feel so good to feel the wind as I bike and run. I can't wait!

The excitement made it hard to settle my nerves, but I made it into bed anyway. HOLY SHEETS! The bed was so soft. The fabric felt slippery, like I was being caressed by wind as it blew silk around my body, wrapping me in a cocoon. I was afraid I was too excited to fall asleep, but with that thought, I was out.

When 2:30 a.m. arrived, there were three things on my mind: gear, mindset, and warmup. My coach had told me to eat something high in carbohydrates and low in fiber. The goal was to move the food through me before the race and leave minimal substances inside to weigh me down. After the race, I was looking forward to a filling and substantial meal. For two weeks, I'd been eating low insoluble fiber, garbage white bread, and pancakes to clear out my system. I only had to eat one more meal like that.

I was deep within my head, talking to myself.

It's getting too late. I'm going to have to ditch the prep run. But it's not a fail. I'll be okay. It's more important to get my mindset pumped up. Today has to be different from the last time. No comparing yourself with other people, Mark. Enjoy each moment. It's time to celebrate all your hard work.

But as the nervousness set in, my mindset started to waver.

I didn't get my jog in. How on earth did time move so quickly? Well, I have ten minutes before I have to leave. Remember who you are! Yoga always grounds you. Do some yoga.

I tossed down my mat on the hard, unfriendly carpet in the hotel room between the coffee table and the TV. I placed my feet on one end of the mat and tilted my chin down toward my chest. As I inhaled, I lifted my chin off my chest and saw the mat opening up and lengthening much like the hot asphalt of the road would unfold in front of my bike in a few hours. I took another inhalation, lifting my chin higher, and saw the Boulder skyline through the window, still cloaked in night.

Everything was about to come alive. The kinetic energy of the city, the race, and my own emotions were palpable. I basked in it all.

These are the elements I need to cherish today, I reminded myself.

As I got ready to drive to the race, I put my Bluetooth headphones in my ears to listen to just four songs: "We Will Rock You," "We are the Champions," "Another One Bites the Dust" (all by Queen), and the classical "Le Reve D'une Note" by Riopy.

I had been wearing leggings all morning to stay warm. An added plus was that they hid my shaved legs. But when the race was about to begin, I had to take the leggings off.

Ava is going to look at me with disgust and ridicule when she sees my legs, I thought. *But that's okay. Be proud of who you are and who you have become.*

Sometimes, when we catastrophize, we're right. When Ava saw my legs, a shadow moved across her face as if a bit of life had been ripped from her. She didn't have the usual radiance when she looked at me. I hoped that look wouldn't stick. It made me feel dirty, as I had so often in my life.

But then, I was able to shift my mindset again. I rejected that dirty feeling. I instantly became proud and felt that I almost had the strength to come out of the closet.

If I'm able to cross that finish line, I'll know it's possible.

It was the largest crowd I'd ever seen gathered together for the same goal. Tears formed in my eyes as I realized how this crowd was similar to the sober and gay communities. To be in the presence of so many men and women who had sacrificed so much to get there was tremendously humbling. Many of them had worked harder than me. Some had already completed several triathlons and would go on to finish two or three more races before the year was over. I felt like I was part of a pack of people with one body and one breath—thousands of us huddled together in tight wet suits just waiting to express ourselves in the way we had fought for tooth and nail. If training is the sketch, and the gear is the paintbrush, the masterpiece would be our time to shine while racing.

10-9-8-7-6-5-4-3-2-1 ...

The first gun went off, and the fastest of swimmers took to the water. A buzzer sounded every five seconds, and another wave of brave souls then plunged into the water. Each wave made my heart beat louder, stronger, and faster.

Finally, my wave was next, and a stillness permeated my soul. I looked at the man next to me and said, "Here we are, my friend. Let's rock this thing." He nodded, acknowledging my excitement, and the buzzer went off.

My reflexes kicked in, and off I went with high knees busting through the shallow waters and a final all-out leap with my arms forward, my chin tucked, and my legs jutting out behind me into a dive.

The water, slightly cold, sent a response to my brain to tense up. It's important to tear down that wall immediately and let the magic happen. I knew from experience that otherwise, I would tire within a few minutes. Rather than waiting for fatigue to debilitate me, I acted with inaction and waited until the neural response settled down.

By slowing my swim significantly for a moment, I allowed a few swimmers to take the lead, but I was fine with that. The morning sun glistened across the water, as the swimmers churned, breaking through the color. I chose to enjoy the moment like a conductor during the big show. It was my time to express myself as the triathlete I had become. So I took each stroke as if it were a graceful brush breaking through the canvas of the sunrise.

Since I smiled and enjoyed every moment, unlike my prior attempt, I got through the swim with flying colors and readied for the bike. When I climbed on, I quickly summoned a mindfulness technique I'd learned. The reward was freely breathing in oxygen, unlike the restricted breaths in the swim. If I could keep my thoughts on the simple things, the bike portion would go well.

During this part of the race, I had to fight my natural will and desire to push too hard. If I did, I wouldn't finish. Since biking at a pace below my threshold is boring to me, I had to trust the limits my coach had given me and try to appreciate the small things.

You have fifty-six miles of this, Mark. The small things will add up and keep you from boredom. Feel the wind across those sexy, smooth legs.

I laughed and kept peddling. Along the way, riders passed by while I left others in my dust. We all exchanged encouragement for one another. It felt like we were warriors all fighting the same battle, pulling each other up and driving each other forward. It was magnificent to feel that together. I recognized how my grandiose superiority complex in prior races had held me back from both performance and gratification in the race.

Nearly two hours later, I finally approached the transition area where I switched from biking mentality to the bare bones: running, the most primal part of a triathlon.

The run was where I'd find out if I had been true to myself, trusted my coach, and had faith in my training. If any of those were lacking, I wouldn't finish.

It was the last stroke of the brush and the final gloss, the last chance to render all the hard work a masterpiece or a waste. At this point of endurance racing, the animal is caged, and the machine is unleashed. As a long, steady, ache settles in during the run, many thoughts can penetrate the mind and easily make or break you. You have to get through them or get off the pot.

People overheat. They cramp. They get hauled to the hospital with dehydration, irregular heartbeat, or other cardiac events. The run is no joke.

About halfway into the run, I realized I'd come up short in many ways. But I was determined to grow from my mistakes rather than dwell on them. "We are the Champions" played in my head. I'd made mistakes but would come through. *Thanks, Freddie Mercury!*

I heard the finish line before I saw it, starting as a gentle hum and slowly turning into a roar. That sound pulled me in like a temptation and dragged me through time, causing me to forget my pain and my will. Then, I saw it—the finish line.

Suddenly, every ache, tear, bead of sweat, and fear that I had experienced came back full throttle. But the lyrics that Freddie sang in my head allowed me to hold my head high. I let out a scream as I used the words of the song to break through the pain. I felt like all my sins were stapled to my chest, exposing me bare—the real me, no apologies.

With the finish line a mere couple of feet in front of me, I was once again graced by the welcoming arms of unity, and I accepted them by lifting my arms up to the sky. We had all faced our demons. We had risen above. We had come so far.

A man hugged me before I fell over. Then, he lifted me up and told me to keep walking or I'd cramp. I got myself back up and followed his directions. Regardless of where I placed, I felt like a champion. I had conquered my own demons and accomplished something that was beyond meaningful for someone who had spent so many years enveloped in self-destruction.

Remember this, I told myself. *Remember who you are.*

I now keep a sticky note on my wall that's the first thing I see every morning. It contains three words that mean the world to me: *Remember the Run.*

I had just one more hurdle because it was clear to me: if I was going to feel like a champion, I had to live like one. And there's no room for lies in a champion's life.

I had seen the film *Bohemian Rhapsody* about Freddie Mercury and Queen three times over the two months before the race. There's a scene in which he returns from the band's first American tour to find his wife distraught. Freddie had been acting detached. After a few minutes of nail-biting anticipation, he says to her, "I'm bisexual."

She tells him she can't stay with him because he's "gay."

But he told her he was bisexual. Why did she take it to the next level?

Honestly, I wish Ava had taken it to the next level. I didn't have the strength to say I was gay the first time around. I would have saved us so much heartache if I had that strength.

After that scene in the movie, I always say, "Freddie, good sir, I understand the challenge."

You're gay, and it's time to accept it, I told myself.

THIRTY-TWO

LIVING MY TRUTH

For most of my life, I felt like I was in the wrong place doing the wrong thing, but I had never felt that more so than in my marriage to Ava. This new me didn't feel right with Ava, and she no longer felt right with me.

Not long after the triathlon, she started to come home late, smelling like booze. I no longer wanted to hide myself, so I didn't.

I met up with a tall man of Latin descent, and I felt the strong sexual desire and drive of manhood engulf me and wrap me in. Warm and lustful, I fell into his kisses. Historically, I would have felt guilty immediately after, but not this time. I basked in the experience, and afterwards, I didn't feel bad about it. I was finally ready to come all the way out, once and for all.

Later that evening, I put the baby to bed and creeped across the creaky floorboards into the living room where Ava was holding my phone, looking at messages that seemed to indicate an affair. She glared at me with the same look as on race day when she saw my shaved legs. She asked me if I had anything to say. I was devastated that I would have to come out to her in this way.

"Ava, I'm gay," I said quietly.

"What?!" she cried out. "I thought you were bi!"

"I did, too. It has taken me a long time to sort this out, but I can't deny it any more. I've never been bi, and I've always been a long way from straight."

She paused and looked at me for a second. Then, she laughed. "You're not gay."

"Yes, Ava, I am," I said resolutely.

The ensuing moments were much quieter than I had expected. She just said, "get out" over and over.

It was final. I didn't belong anymore.

I hopped into my truck that was covered with a few inches of heavy snow. Without my prompting, the music started playing. It startled and angered me. Earlier in the day, I had been ecstatic as I blared the tunes of 1990s teen pop stars—the ones I'd always been ashamed of liking. But now, sheer panic and grave remorse filled every bone in my body. There was no music fit for such dark times.

I turned the music off quickly and watched as the snow began melting on my windshield. I rubbed my hands together fiercely and blew warm air on them. *What the fuck am I going to do now?* I asked myself.

Immediately after the race, I felt a surge of power, strength, and confidence. But I didn't use it to fuel instant action like I should have. . I still longed to be straight—to be "normal" with my "normal family." I wanted to be a happy father with a beautiful wife and two gorgeous boys. I wanted to be like I envision the lives of straight people—real, authentic, pure. I had never had that. I'd never felt real. I'd never felt authentic. I'd certainly never felt pure. I had never belonged.

The snow cascaded down in chunks from my windshield. It was clear enough to drive, so I started down the street. We lived on a highway, but I wished the speed limit was fifteen miles per hour because I wanted to continue to drag my feet.

As I drove down the road, significantly slower than the speed limit, partly due to weather but mostly due to my mood, my face felt hot and red. Still, a shiver rose up through my bones. This shiver was a familiar feeling. I used to get it before meeting with a guy. It wasn't a good feeling. It felt wrong, like I'd done something bad.

That particular night, however, I didn't have the introspective acumen to turn away from the shiver and deal with it in a healthy way. So I drove to a gay men's sex club. An alcoholic knows, as did I, that there had to be a more wholesome solution to calm the shivers. But history has shown that time and time again, habit outweighs rationality, especially when someone is tired and emotional.

The shivers ran deep, and the sweat began to build up under my armpits. I used the anticipation like a horse at the starting gate. My speed increased as I began filling my mind with sexual fantasies. Soon, I could be where I belonged. A smug smile filled my face, and the snow flew past me like stars while I drove through the darkness. I almost felt like a Jedi ready to defect the force and the good he'd always known.

I have nowhere to go anyway, I justified to myself as I sat in the parking lot trying to settle my nerves. I hated walking in all shaky like some strung-out addict. *I've come this far, so I might as well go in.*

Snow whistled by me as I slid my body out of the truck and slammed the door quickly to keep the snow from getting inside. I swung the door of the club open, and the front desk guy grinned at me like a candy shop owner when a school bus pulls up. *I guess I'm welcome. Good choice*, I thought.

After checking in and paying my fee, the door unlocked with a loud clank, similar to the sound of a jailhouse door being disarmed. That was my cue. I walked in and stood a foot inside the door, turning my head to the left and to the right. It was so dark in both directions that it seemed only a bat could navigate the room.

As my eyes adjusted, I slowly walked down the hallway, passing closed doors from which I heard deep and melodious sexual moaning.

At the end of the hallway, I found a locker room with more light. I stripped off my clothes because that's what you do at this place. I grabbed a towel from the rack and flung it over my shoulder. I felt free. There hadn't been many times in my life that I'd felt free to be naked around other people. I had always been too scared of people thinking I was gay. But in this place, it didn't matter.

This feels good. I finally belong, I thought as I neared the bath house area where men were congregating. I rounded the corner and saw a neon-lighted pool and hot tub with leather swings around it. There were also booths with holes on each side. If there was one thing I remembered from my drug-induced prostitution days, it was how these places felt, functioned, and smelled. My now sober self, however, wasn't filled with the same feelings I had back then.

Instead, I looked around and realized I had nothing to gain in this place. I felt like I was standing at a familiar bar ordering drinks, but I finally had an ID with my real picture on it. I remembered the pang of pride I felt when I finally beat the shakes and tremors from alcohol withdrawal through healthy behaviors like exercise and good food. As I stood there watching men grope each other and moan, a similar feeling came over me. I already knew this part of the gay world all too well, and it wasn't the right place for me, at least not right then.

So I returned to the locker room and put my clothes back on. When I got back to my car, I decided to call a friend who had been helping me come out. I told him about the sex club incident and how I was feeling.

"Sex has its place in the gay world," he said, "just like it does in the straight world, but you've got to find yourself in the gay world first."

"A lot like being a teenager again, huh?"

"Yes, exactly."

"Well, it's a good thing I'm not tempted to use again."

"Yes, drugs and alcohol are the fate of many new gay men, and I'm so happy to hear you're solid in your sobriety. It's going to make it easier."

"Maybe tomorrow, you can help me dress because I'm really ready to stop wearing baggy jeans and flannels all the time!"

He laughed. "That's more like it. Let's get out there and be gay and find your inner boy!"

Finding my boy. Now, that thought set well with me. I had always wanted to feel like other boys. I had looked up to my male friends. I admired them and wanted to be like them. I tried desperately to act like them, hoping it would help me feel "normal" and help me to like "normal" things. But I never did.

One place where I knew I could try on "my new boy" was in my sober group. I didn't feel 100% safe there, but with their help, I had overcome what I had once believed impossible: *sobriety*.

The difficult issue about my group was that it was all men, about forty guys in their mid-to-late forties and up. I had never felt comfortable to be myself around other men. I'd always been so self-aware of my presentation as a man that it could easily be confused with narcissism. Gay jokes in the group weren't uncommon, and the guys were as crude as sailors. They talked about dick and pussy so much that it made me more uneasy than I'd felt in high school.

Still, I had learned in my recovery that I was safe to share anything in the group. I had gone back after full-blown relapses, still smelling like booze. I had gone back thirty minutes after leaving jail while still tripping on acid. I had gone back after trying to kill myself. I had shared my weaknesses time and again, crying in the arms of the support there like a baby at his mother's bosom. The sober group had become the perfect place for me to try truth-telling. It was the first place I found where telling the truth was seen as confident, and telling the truth was what saved your life.

So what did I have to lose? Maybe a few older men would laugh at me? I didn't care. *I can do this*, I assured myself.

I walked into the meeting, sweating through my winter jacket. I heard "Good morning, Mark," but I didn't respond cordially as usual. I was too tense.

I simply said "Hi" and avoided eye contact.

God, I can't believe I'm about to do this. But I can't wait to get this out of me. Am I really doing this? I need to go to the bathroom. I can't handle the small talk.

I went into a stall and began scrolling on my phone, waiting for the meeting to start so that I could finally rip the closet doors off of me. My heart was pounding into my throat, and my hands sweated so much that my phone couldn't recognize the strokes of my fingers.

When the familiar silence came over the building, that was my cue. I came out of the bathroom, fitting into my role as faithful, committed attendee, but this particular day, I was there for no one but myself. I had to come out in order to survive. If I didn't do it that morning, I knew I would be drunk by noon. So I took my seat with my face as hot as a wood stove.

The opener was always, "Does anyone have any topics they'd like to discuss?"

That was what I was waiting for. If you spoke up during this time, it was expected to be something juicy.

"Anyone?" he asked again.

Silence fell across the room. No one had a topic, and mine burned like a ghost pepper on the tip of my tongue.

"Okay, then, why don't we read something from the book."

"Actually," I broke in before the section of the book was chosen by one of the men who had been in the room for forty-plus years and knew everything backwards and forwards.

"Well, it's not really a topic," I continued. "But I have something to say. It's something I've wanted to say my whole life. If I've learned anything from being here these past few years, it's that you guys can handle it and can help me with it. It's my biggest fear—the largest reason for my drinking and drug use. It's the reason my wife and I are separated."

I knew I was dragging on and trying to avoid actually saying it, and as I looked around, I saw that I was beginning to lose their attention. So I just blurted it out: "I'm gay, and if I didn't say that today, I was going to leave this room and drink. I'm gay, and it's so fucking scary to tell you guys this."

My eyes darted across the forty faces in the room, and my gaze landed somewhere in the corner of the ceiling like I was looking for a fly. When I heard nothing, my eyes relaxed, and I looked back down. No one was laughing. No one was even smiling smugly or making jokes. They weren't even staring at me. From across the room, a fella I had mentored broke a smile when our eyes met. He looked at me like I had just saved his kids from a kidnapper.

"It's because of things like this that I come to this meeting," an old man finally said from the corner of the room. He had never missed a day for decades.

"The bravery Mark just showed is what keeps me sober," another chimed in.

"Can I give you a hug?" the man directly next to me said as he stood up. Then, a few more of them came over to embrace me.

"I knew I could trust you guys, but with all of your cock jokes, you sure didn't make it easy," I admitted.

Everyone laughed, and the meeting resumed. Within moments, my topic became a thing of the past, and my shoulders dropped what felt like a foot.

I was finally free to be *my boy*. I had only begun to feel that freedom, and suddenly, I felt it in the midst of forty manly men. It was extraordinary, but it also felt normal and right.

Just as when I tried on my first speedo and shaved my legs also felt normal and right. Just as when I trained hard, it felt normal and right. Just as when I flirted with other men, it felt normal and right. It took so long to get there because first, I had to experience those things. Until I did—through triathlon and sobriety—there was no chance of coming out.

Over the next few months, I overhauled my wardrobe and began taking part in gay and sober groups. I went to potlucks and met up with other gay men for coffee and dinners. I built connections and freely disclosed myself and my struggles. I tried to humble myself to a community I knew very little about. Due to my homophobia, I had built a fortress to protect myself. So I tried to learn as much as I could about the community I was joining. This approach made coming out a lot easier. In fact, everyone in my life began supporting me more than I could have imagined.

Even my ex-wives. Shortly after I moved my belongings into a nearby apartment, Ava and Callie moved in together so that we could raise the boys as a solid unit. They continue to work hard at forgiving me, and I continue to work hard at being authentic and true to them.

It has finally become clear to me that living any lie is more painful than any truth. And these two women in my life have been magnanimous enough to realize that forgiveness weighs less than resentment.

The pain I caused them as a result of my lies is enough to warrant their rejection of me, but they both fight to accept me on a daily basis. Because of their strength, the foundation for something beautiful has been set, and much love has been able to blossom between all of us. I admire them both very much, and I'm enormously grateful for them. While I know I have many apologies to make to them and to others, and I know I can't make up for all I've done, I can start by becoming the best father I can be for my sons.

When I came out to my parents, they didn't react as I thought either. Their marriage showed the depths of their ability to love, but I imagined that coming out would strain the cords of that love until it quivered and popped. I had assumed that a lifetime of conservative Southern Baptist heritage would pry them away from me. I couldn't have been more wrong.

They did express some hesitation at first, however.

"I love you, Mark, but I will never support you" were the words that came across the dinner table and hit me in the face like a blindside slug in a sparring match. Everything in me wanted to get up, throw a plate at them, and hiss some hateful words. I wanted to say, "I knew it. I knew you guys would hate me and leave me alone. This is why I didn't come out earlier. I knew it!"

But I also knew that rather than use my hurt to fuel anger, I could use it to bond with them further. I chose the latter, and what happened next was magical.

"I understand. I've spent my whole life not supporting this. I've hated myself for so many years for being gay. But I'm broken, Mom and Dad. I can't do it anymore because it's come to the point that I either go back to drugs and alcohol and slowly or quickly kill myself, or I finally accept myself. This is my rock and hard place. I have no choice."

I then invited them into a discovery. "This is all new to me, too. I'm scared, and I would rather not walk alone. I don't even know what it means to be gay. I do know it isn't a lifestyle of parties, drugs, and orgies. I know it doesn't mean I have to give up my faith and my values. Would you guys just be willing to walk together with me so that we can all learn?"

When their little boy asked for a simple hand in his quest to understand what gay meant, they agreed. A couple of days after that conversation, a wonderful opportunity came for us to search our hearts and minds together. I had written Ryan's parents for permission to use his name and story in my book, and they responded. Little did I know that they had been featured in a recent documentary called *For They Know Not What They Do*. It's a look into the discrimination and subsequent treatment of "deviant" sexual behavior across the evangelical Christian faith.

About ten minutes into watching the film together, my mother's hand reached over toward mine. Out from the safety, warmth, and comfort of her husband's embrace, she took her gay son's hand and held it as if I was just coming to life, and she was pulling me from the womb. You know when a hand conveys feeling because of its strange ability to be so gentle and strong at the same time. With all her love and all her might, she softly wrapped her fingers around mine, and tears began falling from my eyes.

The story of Ryan's tragic death unfolded on the screen, and we all cried together. We also saw stories of great survival that occurred when families came together rather than fight. We saw stories of hope and deepening relationships. We saw love and victory through coming out and being supported.

After the movie, I told my parents the story of my involvement with Ryan. It's slightly different from the movie since I had never told anyone what happened between us. After all, it would have outed me. I was acutely aware that I could have been dead, too, so easily—not because of my addictions per se, but because of my need to lie. A warm glow of gratitude swept through me.

In that film, we all saw what was possible if we came together and used this story to inspire hope. We embraced each other, and I have felt tremendously supported ever since.

Of course, I also worried about what my friends would think. I had felt similarly when I finally admitted to them that I was an alcoholic. I thought everyone would leave me. But all of my friends expressed their gratitude. They could see how much I was hurting, and most of them left me alone because they couldn't watch me abuse drugs and alcohol anymore. I got tremendous support from them in a charity I created for my first triathlon and countless words of admiration. Their messages made my drive stronger as I worked on my sobriety and training.

So when I finally came out to them, the same happened. Nearly all of the guys laughed and said something along the lines of, "Man, I wish you had done that sooner so that more of the girls would have been available!" Meanwhile, my lovely female friends and ex-girlfriends only became closer friends—as if that's what we were intended to be the whole time.

My relationships, both with men and woman, are so much less confusing now. Before, navigating relationships was like walking through a lava field, jumping from rock to rock, unsure if it was going to collapse into flames or find safe footing. After coming out, it was like walking in a field of fresh strawberries where you know that no matter which berry you eat, it isn't going to be poisonous.

Pretty quickly after coming out, I discovered that sex didn't define me or my gay identity. There's no guilt attached to sex anymore because I know I'm not wrong or dirty for liking men. A couple of times, I've gone to big parties and danced late into the night while wearing minimal clothing, but I didn't have to drink or use drugs. I was finally comfortable enough in my skin to enjoy dancing for dancing, people for people, and love for love.

My gayness, I realized, is about being free to be myself, and that's all. It's actually pretty simple.

I've been so lucky to have been given so much support since I've come out. I wish I had known long ago that it was available to me. When I came out to my sober group and the other people in my life, I learned that if we let people in, they will often offer us acceptance and love. Even when someone doesn't think they have people around them who will accept them, there are online groups that can provide the acceptance they need. There *is* support available if we look for it and allow people to give it to us.

But no matter what anyone else felt about me, it was me who had to learn how to accept myself and forgive myself. That is an inside job.

Author Shannon L. Alder has said, "We are all lies waiting for the day when we will break free from our cocoon and become the beautiful truth we waited for."

I'm still very much a work in progress. But after all I've been through and all I've done, I can honestly say that I'm now proud of who I am in every area of my life.

Resources

Topics in this book include:

- PTSD and other trauma
- Addiction
- Suicidal Ideation and Suicide attempts
- Mental Health Issues
- Gang related crimes
- Rehab
- Sober Living Arrangements
- LGBTQ Coming Out
- Gender Identity Confusion
- Prostitution and Unprotected Sex
- Heroin and opioid dependency
- Prescription drug use/abuse
- Benzodiazepine dependence
- Alcohol abuse
- Intravenous Drugs

If you or a loved one need help with any of these topics please refer to this resource page:

www.markaturnipseed.com/resources

Acknowledgments

Besides the groups I mentioned in the Introduction, this book is also for another crowd. It's for all those who no longer tell lies and were strong enough to help me realize that I no longer needed to live a lie.

This book is for Kergan and Russ, who helped me accept who I am with pride.

It's for Jim, who helped me begin my recovery from addiction.

It's for my mother and father, who always believed in me.

It's for my ex-wives, Ava and Callie, who fought hard for me and showed me that I was worth fighting for.

It's for my sons, River and Elliott, who show me daily that it's okay to live with honesty, innocence, and curiosity.

Finally, it's for my God and my heart's savior, Jesus Christ, for whom all this good credit is due.

INTEGRITY | ENDURANCE
COACHING

INTEGRITY ENDURANCE COACHING

The opioid crisis is an international pandemic. Addiction is the chronic disease that drive the crisis and improved medication/therapy adherence is missing link in a more well rounded treatment.

Integrity Endurance seeks to improve adherence by implementing a program of health, wellness and fitness by connecting opioid addicts in treatment with personal trainers and health and wellness coaches.

Get Involved

www.integrityendurance.com

MARK ADAMS TURNIPSEED

Fitness coach and LGBTQ addiction recovery advocate Mark A. Turnipseed is the author of *My Suicide Race: Winning Over the Trauma of Addiction, Recovery, and Coming Out*.

Focused on good health, self-acceptance, and authenticity, Mark shares how you can tap into your best self through the daily practice of compassion and self-acceptance. Sharing his own recovery story to inspire and motivate others, Mark discusses the health-focused tools he has used to overcome addiction, take on a rigorous triathlon, and embrace aspects of himself that caused him shame from age six until adulthood. As a keynote speaker and workshop leader, Mark speaks to recovery groups and gay communities about Fitness as a Recovery Tool, Checking In on

Sober Health, and When Good Health and Wellness Means Coming Out. In his work with Integrity Endurance, Mark helps those recovering from addiction navigate their personal endurance and fitness journeys by connecting them with fitness and wellness resources for holistic and balanced health.

For booking and additional information visit:

www.markaturnipseed.com

Twitter: @markaturnipseed

Instagram: @markaturnipseed

Facebook: @markaturnipseed

Made in the USA
Monee, IL
06 August 2021

75084554R10142